Give Me the Book!

Give Me the Book!

THE STORY OF SAM COCHRAN AND LIGHT FOR THE LOST

HOLY BIBLE

by **CHUCK FREEMAN**
and **BOB BURKE**

Commonwealth
PRESS
Oklahoma City, Oklahoma

foreword by everett stenhouse

Give Me The Book!

THE STORY OF SAM COCHRAN AND LIGHT FOR THE LOST

First Edition Copyright 2002 by
Light for the Lost
1445 N. Boonville Avenue
Springfield, Missouri 65802-1894

By Chuck Freeman and Bob Burke

Design and production by Sandi Welch/2W Design Group;
   Oklahoma City, Oklahoma
Cover illustration by Gil Adams; Tulsa, Oklahoma

Library of Congress Catalog Card Number

ISBN #0-9645140-1-X

Printed in the United States of America

Contents

Acknowledgements

WE ARE ETERNALLY GRATEFUL TO MANY PEOPLE for helping make this book possible. Sam and Geri Cochran and their children opened their hearts and boxes of photographs to allow us to tell the story properly.

LFTL National Coordinator Benny Ferguson and Heather Scranton, Waketa Williams, and Becky Harp of his staff, encouraged and assisted in tracking down old photographs and research materials.

Wayne Warner, director of the Flower Pentecostal Heritage Center, the archives of the Assemblies of God, fully cooperated in our quest for documentary evidence of the growth of Light for the Lost. Glenn Gohr, certainly one of the nation's finest Pentecostal archivists and researchers, spent dozens of hours at the Flower Center scanning old copies of *The Pentecostal Evangel* and other publications for references to Sam and Light for the Lost.

Robert Burke, Eric Dabney, Jerry Freeman, Stephanie Ayala, and Amy Burke Nicar helped with research, photography, and transcription of interviews. Aleda Swartzendruber did a masterful job of editing the manuscript.

Essential to the success of this effort were the dedicated friends of Sam and Light for the Lost who reviewed the manuscript and made helpful suggestions. Reviewers included Benny Ferguson, Gary Davidson, Dwain Jones, Don Jacques, Jerry Freeman, Wayne Warner, Glenn Gohr, Frank and Linda Cargill, Mart Green, Lindell Warren, David Hodges, Steve Dow, Robert Burke, Billy Brummett, Armon Newburn, Phil Taylor, Wayne Long, Colen Lassiter, Greg Whitlow, Jim McNabb, Loren Triplett, Al Perna, Jr., John Bueno, and Sam and Geri's wonderful children.

Thanks to Sandi Welch for her creative genius of design and layout of the book. And, we thank Almighty God for laying the vision for the lost of the world on Sam Cochran's heart. Otherwise, this story would never have been told.

CHUCK FREEMAN
BOB BURKE
2002

Foreword

MANY STERLING WORDS COULD BE USED to describe Sam Cochran. First, he is a Christian. Those of us who have the privilege of knowing him well certainly know that. In our decades-long friendship I have had the personal pleasure of sharing missionary conferences, Light for the Lost banquets, kneeling together at many altars, as well as spending days together on a fishing boat in Mexican waters. Whenever or whatever, Sam is always a Christian.

He is an excellent lay-preacher and has inspired thousands in churches and conferences across the nation. Sam is a faithful father and husband. He is loved by his children and adored by Geri, his wife of more than half a century.

Sam has served on church boards and is a true pastor's friend. He has earned well the reputation of being a pillar of the church. Sam is a businessman and has been highly successful in all of his enterprises.

In addition to all the above, Sam Cochran has always been a visionary. And from all of those early dreams and visions there arose out of the dust of the defeats and the glow of the successes the finest and most effective layman's ministry known to the Christian Church worldwide today. The passion of his soul has been that every person on earth be given a presentation of this glorious gospel story in printed form. This is the heartbeat of the man who has shown us compassion for the lost.

Sam is not content to touch missions with the tips of his fingers. He has exercised his best energies to put his arms around the world. He has always understood clearly the words of the renowned Scottish preacher Robert Murray McCheyne when he said, "We are all here with measured tasks for a measured time."

He also knows that world evangelism can never be accomplished by professional missionaries or by paid nationals. The task is simply too great. Enter Light for the Lost! Sam's soul was pierced through by the glaring inequities in gospel distribution over the world.

When Sam was storming over the country in those early days of Light for the Lost, praying, plodding, and pleading for the printed gospel, the Communists were printing annually two pieces of Communist literature for every person on earth. Is there wonder at the words of the grandson of Mahatma Ghandi when he said, "The missionaries taught my people to read but they have let the Communists give my people something to read." The revolutionaries boasted of the China revolution to communism, "We took China by the printed page."

The fact that the Christian world possessed almost all Christian literature was unacceptable to Sam Cochran. He pored over the astronomical statistics with regards to the people still outside the circle of effective gospel witness. I've listened to this man with a sword in his soul, pleading with congregations to put their ear to the ground and listen to the cries of the damned over the world.

Thomas a'Kempis said, "I would rather exercise faith than know the definition thereof." That is Sam! "Let's get on with it! Don't just talk about it! Let's do it!" And, as they say, the rest is history. Light for the Lost literature has led millions up Calvary's hill to kneel at the foot of the Cross.

We have heard you, dear friend and brother, Sam Cochran, and we pledge our best efforts to keeping the vision of Light for the Lost alive and effective.

EVERETT STENHOUSE
*Former Assistant General Superintendent
of the Assemblies of God*
2002

Speak and I will answer, "Lord send me."

—FROM THE TRADITIONAL HYMN

one
The Vision

HIS HANDS WERE STRETCHED TOWARD HEAVEN. Tears streamed down young Sam Cochran's face as he lay prostrate on the floor at the altar at First Assembly of God in Santa Ana, California. It was a Sunday night in 1952 that would change the history of evangelism in the last half of the 20th century.

Sam had gone to the altar because of a stirring message that made him want to accomplish more for his Lord's Kingdom. As he was praying, a calmness came over him. It was as if a movie projector was turned on and scenes began playing out in front of him. What he saw shook his heart deeply.

There was a great multitude of people standing, looking up. A large hand out of heaven held a Bible toward the throng. The men and women reached as far as they could, desperately stretching their hands toward the Bible. In unison, the mass of humanity cried, "GIVE ME THE BOOK! GIVE ME THE BOOK! GIVE ME THE BOOK!"

Sam Cochran, at age one, in 1926. His intense personality was evident from childhood.

However, just as the hand and Bible came down, a trap door opened beneath them. Flames and smoke shot into the air as the people dropped into the screaming pit, lost for eternity.

The meaning of the vision was perfectly clear. Sam knew that God's purpose for his life was to the send the Word of God to every soul on earth as long as he had breath. He had no idea how his mission would be accomplished, but he promised God he would do his best.

Sam arose from the altar with a renewed dedication, indeed a passionate burden, to bring light to the lost millions of the world. At that moment, one of the most successful missions programs in history was born.

Samuel V. Cochran was born April 20, 1925, on a farm outside Santa Ana, California. He was blessed with godly parents. Henry

Henry Augustus "Gus" Cochran and Mary Ethel Turner Cochran, Sam's parents, on their 50th wedding anniversary.

Augustus "Gus" Cochran farmed from dawn to dusk, raising fruit and vegetables in the rich soil of southern California. Gus Cochran was a descendant of the Earl of Dundonald, chief of the Cochran Clan in Scotland.

Sam's mother, Mary Ethel Turner Cochran, was so sick after Sam's birth that her sister-in-law, Sadie Turner, had to stay with the family to take care of her until Sam was two years old. Without the help of his wife to run the farm, Gus Cochran moved his family in 1926 to nearby Anaheim, to a plot of land across the road from where Walt Disney would build Disneyland three decades later.

The Cochrans were God-fearing, church-going people. They were charter members of and regularly attended First Assembly of God in Santa Ana. They strongly believed in the doctrines of the Assemblies of God, a fellowship formed in 1914 when 300 Pentecostal leaders met in Hot Springs, Arkansas, with a God-endorsed idea of banding together splinter groups of Pentecostals to increase their world missions efforts.

Gus and Ethel Cochran accepted the major tenants of faith of the Assemblies of God, especially the belief that the infilling of the Holy Spirit, or "receiving the baptism in the Holy Ghost," was a separate and distinct experience that followed salvation. The "Baptism" was controversial because the Assemblies of God believed that its initial evidence was the speaking in "tongues," or an unknown heavenly language.

The Cochrans enjoyed the Pentecostal style of singing and worship. They took Sam to Sunday School and practiced what they preached. They depended upon God for their very existence and prayed for guidance in front of their children. Daily readings from the Bible were standard operating procedure in the Cochran household.

Sam began his formal education at nearby Katella Elementary School in Anaheim. He walked through orange orchards to get to school. When the family moved from the farm into Santa Ana, Sam attended Franklin Elementary School. He was a good student and excelled in track. In the sixth grade, he won the 50-yard dash in an all-city track meet. His record of 5.8 seconds stood for 14 years.

At age 14, Sam accepted Christ as his personal Savior during a revival at his home church. He played in the band at Santa Ana High School. After classes, he was in charge of street sales for two newspapers, the *Santa Ana Register* and the *Los Angeles Herald*.

A few months before Sam graduated from high school in May 1943, he joined the United States Navy. World War II was raging both in Europe and in the Pacific and Sam felt a strong urge to serve his country. His Navy basic training was in San Diego, California, where he

Sam graduated from Santa Ana High School in 1943. He had already enlisted in the U.S. Navy.

received instruction as a gunner on a 5 x 38, an automatic beach-loaded antiaircraft and surface gun.

Sam shipped out on a Liberty ship as a member of the "armed guard," charged with protecting maritime ships headed for the action in the South Pacific. He became the pointer on the gun, the man who actually pulled the trigger.

His group served valiantly in the Philippines and among the scattered islands of the vast Pacific ocean where American troops fought Japanese soldiers whose leaders were trying to extend their influence over the entire world. Sam made $66 a month as a Navy gunner, serving on a number of different tankers, victory ships, and liberty ships.

Even though Sam had attended an Assemblies of God church almost every Sunday of his life, he had drifted from God. One night, 7,000 miles from home, in the recently liberated Port of Halandia, in New Guinea, he had a special session with God. In a gun enclosure aboard a ship carrying ammunition to American soldiers, Sam was frightened for his life.

Sam loved his country very much and actively sought entry into the armed forces during World War II. He was a Navy gunner for three years. It was during an intense battle that he surrendered his life to Christ.

Bombing and strafing of the dug-in Japanese positions in the mountains above the port continued day and night. The awful noise of the bombs and shells was constant. Navy warships pulled alongside his ship and shelled the mountain strongholds of the enemy. Sam remembered, "As the bullets whizzed past our ship, I knew I could be killed at any moment. I dropped on my knees and began to pray."

Sam promised God that he would serve Him if He got him home safely. God fulfilled His end of the bargain. But Sam did not. He spent the last months of active duty, after the war had ended, managing a Navy hotel

give me the book!

in Peking, China. For his Navy service, Sam was awarded four combat stars and four ribbons.

When Sam came home in 1946, he had a choice of careers. The Maritime Service offered him a commission as a purser if he would return to maritime ships. However, he refused the commission and enrolled at Johnson Business College in Santa Ana. There he met a beautiful young lady he liked very much. A friend told him her name. It was Geraldine "Geri" Kerley.

two

The Ultimatum

SAM HAD GREAT PLANS FOR HIS LIFE, but God was not in them. He was studying accounting and law at Johnson Business College in Santa Ana. He wanted to get an education and go into business, to obtain all the material things he did not have growing up.

The more Sam saw Geri Kerley, the more he liked her. She agreed to a few Coke dates but told him that she wanted a Christian home and that she could not get serious with anyone who did not have the same goal. Sam told Geri he had no time for Christianity. He was headed for a life of business!

Sam ignored Geri's feelings until one weekend when she invited him to a Hyman Appelman revival meeting in a large tent near Anaheim. At first, Sam refused the invitation. Then came the ultimatum. Geri told Sam that unless he went with her to the tent meeting, she would not date him anymore. Sam gave in, but went only to please her because he liked her that much.

Sam and Geri on a date a few weeks before their wedding in 1947.

During the spirited song service, God began reminding Sam of his promises made in the gun enclosure on the frightful night in New Guinea during World War II. The pressure mounted as Brother Appelman told how Christ was nailed to an old rugged cross for Sam's sins. When the altar call was made, Geri reached over and took Sam's hand and asked if he would accept Christ. A Christian worker on the end of the aisle moved toward the young couple and invited them to the altar.

Sam feeds Geri a piece of their wedding cake.

Sam dropped to his knees at the altar and again accepted Christ as his personal Savior and Master of his life. He went to his car and threw away the cigarettes that had bound him since his stint in the Navy.

Six months later, on June 3, 1947, Sam and Geri were married at Gospel Center, a nondenominational church in Santa Ana that Geri attended. When they returned home from a honeymoon in the Redwoods in northern California, they bought a small house in Garden Grove, California, for $7,500.

Sam and Geri graduated from Johnson Business College in 1947. Sam took a job with Sheffield Insurance Agency. He liked dealing with people and learning the insurance business.

Geri was a devout Christian, but was unfamiliar with Pentecostal doctrine and worship. For awhile, she and Sam attended her church, Gospel Center. But when the pastor left, she agreed to attend Sam's church. At first Geri was startled by the worship services at First Assembly of God in Santa Ana. However, she received the baptism in the Holy Spirit within a few months and accepted Pentecost without hesitation.

In 1949, two significant events occurred. Sam, who had built a reputation as a good and sincere insurance salesman, formed his own agency, Sam Cochran and Company. He had developed an impressive list of insurance clients that allowed him to venture out on his own.

But the major event of 1949 was the birth of Sam and Geri's first child, James Lee Cochran, born June 26 in Santa Ana.

The Cochrans outgrew their tiny first home in Garden Grove. They bought a lot and hired an architect to design a new home on North Lynnwood Street in Santa Ana. With a loan from the California Veterans Board, they built a two bedroom, one bath, 938-square-feet house for their growing family. That was all Sam could afford. The insurance business was tough. Some months, the "outgo exceeded the income," Sam recalled.

Sam was active both in his church and in the community. He and Geri rarely missed a church service. Sam was the 1951 president of the Community Chest fund-raising drive in Costa Mesa, California. A second son, Ronald Wayne, was born January 17, 1951. Son Gary Samuel was born in 1958 and the Cochran's only daughter, Susan Elaine, was born December 12, 1955.

During a 1952 revival with evangelist Stanley McPherson at Santa Ana First Assembly, Sam began seeking the Lord in earnest about his specific role in winning the unsaved. After a Sunday night message, Sam went to the altar to pray with another man for a special touch on his life.

Sam was praying "in the Spirit," when he fell "flat on his back." For an hour and 45 minutes, he prayed. Then the vision came.

Sam saw millions of people of every nationality crying, "Give me the Book! Give me the Book! Give me the Book!" But just before the hand of God came down with the Bible, a trap door opened and the people fell into a living, burning hell. Sam heard the cries and screams and saw the flesh and hair burning. In 2001, a half-century after the vision, Sam said he could still smell the burning flesh.

The vision chilled his soul beyond belief. He asked, "God, why are You showing me this?" When he finally came to himself, he realized God had given him a vision. He sat down on the front pew with his pastor, Ben Hardin, and said, "Pastor, I've just had a vision and I don't understand it." Pastor Hardin asked Sam to relate the details of the vision. His advice to Sam was, "You come back to me a year from now and tell me what you've done about the vision and I'll tell you what it meant. Because if you don't do anything about it, it was just a good idea."

Sam did not let the vision die. His burden for the lost of the world grew heavier day by day. On the following Sunday afternoon, he and Geri hosted a half dozen men at their home. Sam took the men aside and told them of his vision. Dr. I.J. Harrison, the president of Southern California Bible College, who had just returned from a missions trip to Guatemala, said thousands of new Christians had nothing to sustain them. The men were touched and agreed with Sam to each give $15 per month to buy copies of the Gospel of John to send to missionaries in Central and South America. Dr. Harrison promised to contact the missionaries.

Other men at the meeting were Paul Klahr, associate pastor of Santa Ana First Assembly; Everett James, a student at Southern California Bible College; Cliff Collins, a local realtor; John Anderson, who worked for a battery company and later founded the American Battery Company; and Dean Burchett, a teacher at Orange Coast College.

Burchett was chosen as chairman of the new group. Everett James was asked to hold services at area churches to raise missions literature funds.

Hollis Lawson was one of the men who caught Sam's vision in its first days. Lawson, who operated a nearby egg-producing ranch, was himself at the altar the night Sam received his life-changing vision. Lawson was among the original six men who pledged a monthly offering to send the Word abroad. The intensity of Sam's burden for the lost was transferred to Lawson who immediately began praying for and financially supporting Sam's vision.

Still Sam was uncertain how God wanted him to fulfill the mission so clearly revealed in the vision. He recalled, "I sought God's will daily. I found that nothing starts itself. One must begin to move forward in the area God wants him to work. When he begins to do that thing, he receives the power to do it. No amount of wishing gets things done, it takes prayer and action."

Sam began talking to his pastor and missionaries about the need for gospel literature on the mission field. He found the need was overwhelming. Missionaries often struggled just to raise budgets to get to a foreign land and secure food and housing for their families. In most cases, there simply was no budget for literature to assist them in spreading the gospel.

Sam was convinced that the written Word was vital to reach the unsaved millions in all parts of the world. He read information about how the Communists were outspending the United States in printing books. A highly educated man from India said, "The missionaries taught my people how to read but they have let the Communists give my people what to read." The rise in world literacy gave the Communists their greatest opportunity. With 15 million people learning to read each year, Sam recognized the urgency of getting the printed Word into the hands of lost men and women. Sam said, "Whoever wins the battle of the books will shape the minds of the people."

Sam agreed with Dr. Oswald J. Smith, a leading authority on world missions, that the only way Christians could "reach every creature" was by means of the printed page. Sam wrote in an early brochure, "Our message must never change. But our method of spreading this message MUST CHANGE or we will doom 1.5 million heathens who have never heard of Christ."

Looking for ways to raise money to pay for printed materials for the mission field, Sam looked to his quartet, the Kingsmen, at Santa Ana First Assembly. Laymen who had joined Sam's efforts pledged their $15 a month for administrative expenses, gas, and oil to transport the quartet to area churches to raise money for missions literature. Original members of the quartet were Sam, Everett James, Dexter Healey, and Dean Burchett. Others who sang in the Kingsmen were Richard Shultz, Danny Thomas, Leroy Bonham, Bill King, Lavonne Kendall, and Terry Shefield.

The first fund-raising service was at First Assembly of God in Anaheim. The offering was only $16.66, but Sam was encouraged as other churches accepted requests for the quartet to sing in exchange for the opportunity to receive an offering for the cause. The first year the Kingsmen raised $392. It was a start. The group handed out membership applications to Kingsmen International,

Sam used the Kingsmen Quartet to get into churches to talk about raising money to send gospel literature to missionaries. Left to right, Sam, Everett James, Richard Shultz, and Leroy Bonham.

the name chose to identify the efforts of the quartet. Money received in services was sent to selected missionaries to pay for copies of the Gospel of John in Mexico. Later, offerings provided Gospels for Central America, Peru, Argentina, and Brazil.

The offerings began to be larger. Sam thought he had hit a gold mine when the people at First Assembly of God in Covina, California, gave $333. Often Sam told the congregation, "If you'll give $100 tonight, we'll give you one of our new records." The Kingsmen had actually recorded an album. One night an old man stood at the rear of the sanctuary and said, "If I don't have to take the record home, I'll give the $100 anyway."

As word about the Kingsmen and their work to raise money for literature for Assemblies of God missionaries spread, Sam needed a more stable organization to handle the distribution of monies received in offerings. The new plan was the formation of the Missionary Gospel Society (MGS) in late 1953.

> *So shall my word be that goeth forth out of my mouth: it shall not return unto me void, but it shall accomplish that which I please, and it shall prosper in the thing whereto I sent it*
>
> (ISAIAH 55:11, KJV).

three

Missionary Gospel Society

ITS OFFICIAL NAME WAS MISSIONARY GOSPEL SOCIETY, Inc., established as a California nonprofit corporation. Extensive bylaws of the new group provided for a National Board of Directors, an annual meeting of the National Council, and defined a "layman" as "any man whose major time is spent in a secular activity from which he derives his major income which is his source of revenue for contributions to the work of the Missionary Gospel Society of the Assemblies of God."

The original idea of using laymen, with pledges of monthly support to pay the administrative expenses of MGS, was an excellent plan. Sam and other supporters could truthfully say that every dime received in offerings at fund-raising services and other events went to purchase literature for missionaries.

The MGS bylaws allowed any district of the Assemblies of God national fellowship to participate as long as each member of the

Everett James, left, was the energetic young Bible school student who recognized the importance of Sam's vision to raise money to send literature to Assemblies of God missionaries. He spent 18 years working directly with Sam in promoting Light for the Lost.

ABOVE: *Sam speaks to an early banquet in southern California.*

RIGHT: *An early brochure promoting the Missionary Gospel Society.*

How many people will have the Word of God because of You?

Every $1.00 provides 1000 with the Gospel Message

Mail your offering today to

Missionary Gospel Society

1786 Newport Blvd.
COSTA MESA, CALIFORNIA

"EVERY CENT PURCHASES GOSPELS"

(Operational Costs Are Paid by the Board of Directors)

Your Missionaries are waiting for "Gospels" to distribute!

WILL YOU HELP TODAY?

LEFT: *Sam at his desk at his insurance office. His bubbling personality and growing knowledge of the insurance business brought him new clients. As God blessed his business, Sam spent more and more time raising money for the Missionary Gospel Society.*

33

District Congress pledged $15 a year. Members of each District Board of Directors were required to pay at least $15 per month.

Sam managed his growing insurance business during the week and spent his weekends promoting the literature project.

Interest in MGS multiplied and enthusiasm spread. The list of churches in California that supported the program grew to 40 by 1955. Total contributions in 1955 jumped to $1,500.

As money was sent to Latin America, testimonies of the value of literature came back. Missionary Arthur E. Lindvall wrote from El Salvador, "Every weekend during Bible school our students went into the little towns nearby and gave a Gospel with their testimony. As a result, 200 were saved in 4 months."

Quentin Shortes, a missionary in Guatemala, wrote, "I was talking to an unbeliever and felt led to give him a New Testament. In 10 days he came to church and testified that he had accepted the Lord by just studying the Testament."

Other missionaries confirmed the great need for an infusion of literature on the field. From British Honduras, A.E. Spence, Jr., wrote, "We need all the gospel literature that we can secure." Ray Morelock, preaching the gospel in Mexico, said, "With our 500 workers we need at least 100,000 Gospels a year."

A valuable member of the MGS team was Everett James, a young Bible school student at Southern California Bible College and member of Sam's quartet, the Kingsmen. Soon James was spending most of his time planning services and other fund-raising events for MGS.

In its third year, 1956, contributions to MGS jumped to $4,000 and Sam realized the operation was getting too big for just the seven men who devoted much of their time to the effort. If Sam's vision was to be completely fulfilled, a more comprehensive program would need to be launched.

Sam turned to the General Council of the Assemblies of God in Springfield, Missouri. By 1956, the capstone of all Assemblies of God achievements was the fellowship's efforts on the foreign mission field. General Superintendent J.W. "Daddy" Welch had written 30 years before about the urgency of missions:

> Anyone who is filled with the Holy Spirit must be a missionary not only in theory but in reality, with a purpose of heart to take or send the light to those who sit in darkness and the shadow of death. This fellowship is and must remain just an agent to spread the gospel to the ends of the earth.

In 1956, the longtime Assemblies of God Director of Foreign Missions, Noel Perkin, entered Sam's life. Perkin had served the Assemblies of God missions program for 30 years. Historian Carl Brumback wrote of Perkin, "He lived, ate, drank, talked, dreamed and sacrificed for missions." One missionary remembered the earpiece on Perkin's glasses was attached with tape for years. Asking Perkin's secretary why the patchwork, she replied, "Brother Perkin so often received urgent and heart-rending appeals from the field for which there were no funds, that he himself would try to meet the need personally; hence, the neglected glasses."

Perkin introduced a new missions strategy for the Assemblies of God in 1957. It was called Global Conquest and represented a shift in missions focus from rural and isolated areas to urban centers. Global Conquest had a three-pronged emphasis; increase the distribution of gospel literature, step up evangelization in key metropolitan centers, and increase efforts to train national pastors and leadership through Bible school programs.

New goals of world missions were announced at the 1957 Assemblies of God General Council. Perkin projected for 1960 an increase of 100 missionaries, above the existing 758; 10,000 national workers; and 600,000 members of the Assemblies of God in foreign lands.

Perkin, like Sam, realized that the need for missions literature was not being met by the national Men's Fellowship Department.

The Cochran children in 1959.
TOP (left to right): *Jim and Ron.*
BOTTOM (left to right): *Sue and Gary.*

Local men's fellowships in Assemblies of God churches raised some money for literature, but the effort was sporadic and not as far-reaching as leadership desired.

Perkin was aware of Sam's success in raising money for literature in California. In 1958, Perkin wrote Sam a letter, inviting him to Springfield to discuss the possibility that the MGS could be a project of the national Assemblies of God Men's Fellowship Department. Perkin was impressed with the early efforts of MGS. He knew that much of the success of Global Conquest rested in raising substantial amounts of money to provide literature for Assemblies of God missionaries.

The Executive Presbytery of the Assemblies of God, the fellowship's governing board, agreed to formally merge its efforts with MGS in July, 1958. In a historic three-page agreement, signed by Noel Perkin and Sam Cochran, the scope of MGS was elevated to that of a national fund-raising program.

The agreement provided that offerings received by the Foreign Missions Department from MGS be deposited in a special account. Sam and the MGS Board of Directors were allowed exclusive control over expenditures from the account. In line with the MGS method of financing the effort, "all costs of travel and support of representatives will be provided from other sources than the offerings given by churches for the purchase of gospel portions and the Scriptures." The new name of MGS was the "Missionary Gospel Society of the Assemblies of God." The initial joint literature project was called "Word for the World." Sam was named national coordinator.

Meanwhile, Everett James had graduated from college and became a licensed minister with the Assemblies of God. As the official MGS field representative, he continued to travel for MGS but based his operations in California. By the end of 1958, MGS had raised more than $30,000 for missions literature. James and Sam received weekly requests from all over the country to speak and introduce the program.

MGS expanded into Oregon. James reported to the board, "God has especially blessed our efforts in the beautiful state of Oregon. In only ten weeks time, He has helped us to produce $2,050 for printed Gospels. We now have a board of 12 men serving in the Oregon District. The national team has held a total of 26 services in Oregon." Oregon elected Homer Moxley as its national MGS representative. Oregon joined two other official MGS districts, Northern California-Nevada and Southern California.

The balance sheet for MGS in July 1959, showed contributions of $4,972 and a $300 loan from Sam. James was paid $200 per month in salary and expenses and used a small office in Costa Mesa.

Logistically, MGS, operating from California, and the association with the Assemblies of God in Springfield, did not make for a smooth operation. Sam and Assemblies of God Men's Fellowship Department officials talked about officially merging the operation in the spring of 1959.

On May 10, 1959, Sam and Everett James flew to Springfield to meet with the Executive Presbytery. Sam wrote of the meeting, "After a stormy trip by air, we arrived in a rainstorm, thankful to God that we arrived. We spent three days in conferences, out of which came the resolution from the Executive Presbytery expressing their desire to merge."

In asking his brethren and supporters to approve the official merger, Sam wrote, "Our national budget, as you can see by the treasurer's report, has now become somewhat like our U.S. government budget. Although not in the red, a greater amount has been spent than our original estimate due to the great increase in travel necessary because of the meeting with the Executive Presbytery and to advise district boards of the results of these meetings."

During the summer of 1959, Sam and many of his closest supporters decided on a name change for the Word for the World project. After much prayer and discussion, the name "Light for the Lost" was chosen. In literature, the program's name was shortened to LFTL.

The National Men's Fellowship Missions Council met at the El Rancho Motel in Millibrae, California, on September 26, 1959. Before the election of officers, Sam served as chairman of the meeting. Present were Dean Burchett of the Southern California District, Ben Kelterborn of the Northern California-Nevada District, Everett James, and Jim Scoggins. Homer Moxley of the Oregon District could not attend the meeting because of bad weather.

The Council raised James' salary as national field secretary to $430 monthly. Lowell Prinzing was appointed as national field representative, provided that sufficient funds were available to pay his salary. A Gospel disbursement committee, consisting of Sam and Burchett, was created to make decisions on expenditures from the Light for the Lost account in Springfield. Burchett was selected as chairman of the Council. Moxley and Kelterborn were elected vice chairman and secretary-treasurer, respectively.

Sam's vision was alive and well. But it was time to move the heart of the operation to Springfield.

Speak and I will answer. "Lord send me."

—FROM THE TRADITIONAL HYMN

four

Light for the Lost

THE CREATION OF LIGHT FOR THE LOST WAS ANNOUNCED by Assemblies of God National Men's Fellowship Executive Director Charles W.H. Scott in the November 1, 1959, edition of *The Pentecostal Evangel.* Scott wrote, "This new literature project of our Men's Fellowship ties in with the Global Conquest goal of reaching the world for Christ with the aid of gospel literature. There are one million literates each week! These must be provided with gospel literature."

Scott challenged the 9,000 Assemblies of God churches in America to join LFTL, writing, "Through Light for the Lost, the men of our churches accept the challenge to do their part in world evangelization by providing gospel literature for the newly literate to read."

Part of the agreement for the National Men's Fellowship Department to take over complete supervision of LFTL was for

Everett James to move his base of operations from California to Springfield. James was given the new title of national secretary of Light for the Lost. Sam, continuing to live and work in California, accepted the title of national administrator.

The National Men's Fellowship Department did not have sufficient income to pay James' salary. Sam, knowing that God was in the plan, went to his banker to borrow $7,500 to finance the national LFTL office for one year. Sam's insurance business had fallen on hard times and the banker was reluctant to loan such a large amount of money.

The banker asked, "When can you pay this back?" Sam answered, "As soon as possible! God will take care of it." Sam sent the borrowed money to the Assemblies of God headquarters, an action that he repeated the next two years until LFTL began receiving sufficient income to finance the national office.

Sam remembered, "God always took care of us. We were never late on a payment to the bank." One year, Sam received a call from the vice president of one of the insurance companies he represented in his business. Sam thought, "Oh boy, he's gonna fire me." Instead, the executive took him out for lunch. Over cracked crab, a new experience for Sam, the man handed Sam a check for $7,500. The vice president said, "This is your bonus for writing very good business."

Sam quietly thanked God and immediately sent the check to the National Men's Fellowship Department to finance another year of operation of LFTL. From the day Sam sent the $7,500 check to Springfield, his own business began to grow. And, more importantly to Sam, LFTL began to flourish.

In 1960, Howard Scott Bush became executive director of the National Men's Fellowship Department. Bush and Sam became good friends, both passionate about world missions. Together they developed a plan to expand the base for raising monthly pledges to finance the administration of LFTL. A National Light for the Lost Council was created.

Under the new plan, each "councilman" would pay $15 per month. Sam personally recruited 40 councilmen in California within the first few weeks. He and Everett James went to Arizona and added another 15 men. The Wisconsin-Northern Michigan District established LFTL committees.

At first, Assemblies of God churches were less than enthusiastic about asking their men to become LFTL councilmen. At the first national convention in Denver, Colorado, in 1960, only five men representing five Assemblies of God districts were present. Sam and the four other stalwart supporters sat around a table and planned the next year's events.

By the end of 1960, councilmen by the dozens were added monthly. Other Assemblies of God districts created district-wide programs, bringing to a total of seven districts with active LFTL committees. Donald Palmer headed the West Central District. Frank Wortman was chairman of the Arizona District LFTL committee, Norman Underwood headed the effort in the Illinois District, and Floyd Shockley was chairman of the Southern Missouri District LFTL committee. Jim Scoggins and Nick Choco were hired as field representatives.

Sam took his first missionary trip outside the United States in May, 1960. He was part of a group of ministers and laymen led by Howard Bush on a ten-day tour of Mexico, Guatemala, and El Salvador. In Mexico, the team heard reports from a Mexican Army general that gospel literature had allowed him to win a "great number" of his soldiers to Christ.

In El Salvador, Sam and other laymen gave their testimonies to a group of businessmen. Sam told of the night in the gun turret in World War II when he gave his life to the Lord and about his renewal at the Hyman Appelman tent revival. After he finished his testimony, Sam started to sit down. A wealthy coffee plantation owner, Ernest Mac Entrée, stood in front of Sam with tears rolling down his face. He extended his hand to Sam and said, "I want to accept Jesus as my Savior, and serve Him." Sam took the man's hand. As they wept together, Sam led Ernest to Christ.

During the trip, Sam heard countless stories from missionaries about the value of printed materials. Traveling from village to village, he saw many people who had not yet heard the gospel. He remembered, "They were everywhere. The streets of every village and city were filled with people serving false gods of stone. Our hearts ached as we saw them."

Louis H. Hauff of San Bernardino, California, wrote of his experience in *The Pentecostal Evangel*, "We saw the value of literature and Gospel distribution. Our bookstores in Santa Ana, El Salvador, and Guatemala City are eagerly waiting to receive more literature to be used by national pastors."

With the assistance of missionary Walter Haydus and six national ministers, 20,000 pieces of gospel literature were given to Indian pilgrims who had traveled to the Shrine of the Black Christ where they stood in line for hours to kiss the cross of the Black Christ. The literature told them of the living Christ who alone is able to forgive sins.

As Sam and the team members stood in a marketplace in El Salvador handing out Gospel portions, the crowd almost created a riot to obtain the Gospels. The people continued to cry, "Please give me one!" long after the supply of Gospel portions was gone. Sam flew home a changed person. His zeal to put into action the plan God had given him in the vision eight years before was renewed.

The Men's Fellowship Missions Council, at its annual meeting in November 1960, adopted a plan of action to carry LFTL to additional districts and send literature to all points on the globe. It was called Operation Saturation, intended to saturate every country in the world with gospel literature.

The Council instructed Everett James to spend half his time in newly organized districts. The goal was to add at least two new

In a brochure, Sam put forth a strict list of qualifications for men serving Assemblies of God churches. He wrote, "You must purpose in your heart to be loyal. Faithfulness in attendance at all services of the church is an evidence of loyalty. Refuse to be a part of any fault-finding. Such acts will lead to dissatisfaction and uselessness to God."

districts in 1961. The total operating budget for the year was approved for $7,797.

In the December 11, 1960, edition of *The Pentecostal Evangel*, Sam announced a goal for local Assemblies of God churches to raise $20,000 to buy two million Gospels needed by missionaries just in Latin America. He wrote:

> This gospel literature is the ammunition that is needed to fight the forces of Communism and heathenism. Our missionaries are pouring out their lives on foreign fields to combat these evil forces and perform a work for God. The true gospel of Jesus Christ is needed by the world and the printed Gospel portion is one of today's best tools to reach the masses. The least we can do is to provide our missionaries with this tool to help accomplish their task.
>
> Many of our faithful missionaries are carrying on great literature distribution efforts. The nationals are going from door to door in teams giving out gospel literature. Great revivals are springing up and churches are being born because of these campaigns.
>
> The cost of these little printed preachers is very small. Throughout the world, the average cost is $1.00 for 100 printed Gospels. For every 14 cents invested in gospel literature today, a soul is won for Christ.

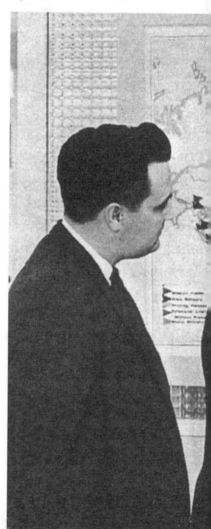

To encourage Assemblies of God men to become more active in their local church, Sam wrote a pamphlet entitled, "How YOU can serve in the Assemblies of God Men's Fellowship." He wrote, "America needs stouthearted men; men who will not count their lives dear unto themselves; men of moral courage, clean men, honest men, men of God...Your talents are needed. Your help is wanted."

Three Assemblies of God leaders discuss Light for the Lost *literature distribution in British Guiana. Left to right, Everett James, the first national LFTL coordinator; C.M. Ward, speaker on* Revivaltime, *the worldwide radio ministry of the Assemblies of God; and J. Philip Hogan, executive director of foreign missions for the Assemblies of God. Courtesy* The Pentecostal Evangel.

In the brochure, Sam outlined the many volunteer positions in local churches, from Sunday School teachers to prayer warriors. He admonished men to let church officers know of their willingness to serve. He said, "You will soon find a place where your life will really count for God."

About the admonition for Christian men to be consistent, Sam wrote, "Be consistent with your daily life so that your testimony will be accepted by others and so win them to Christ. Ask yourself this question, 'If every member of my church were just like me, what kind of church would our church be?'"

With a theme of "Mobilizing Men for Christian Action," LFTL representatives began planting seeds in every Assemblies of God district in the nation. LFTL rallies, featuring steak dinners followed by a stirring message about world missions, raised much-needed funds. Many churches began placing LFTL in their missionary budget and sent monthly offerings. Global-Bank posters appeared in church hallways to solicit monthly freewill offerings.

In 1961, the young, energetic executive director of the Assemblies of God foreign missions program, J. Philip Hogan, began actively promoting LFTL. He wrote, "Already many thousands of dollars have been raised and disbursed through the Foreign Missions Department for this project. The emphatic order the men give us is that we spend the money. As the needs for Gospels arise around the world, we pass these requests on to the Light for the Lost committee and the men invariably come through with the money needed for overseas literature evangelism. Surely the evangelism of this generation demands total commitment by every group in the local church."

Assemblies of God missionaries became increasingly aware of LFTL. By the dozens, they sent their requests to Springfield for money for literature. Earl Taylor, a missionary to Japan, wrote, "The amount of Gospels to be distributed is limited only by the amount of money that can be supplied to us."

Dean Burchett, the chairman of the National Missions Council of Men's Fellowship, challenged Assemblies of God laymen to get involved with LFTL. He said, "In these extremely perilous days the ministry of LFTL is to provide the written Word to bring the lost to Christ, establishing them in the Word. Then, if the missionaries are forced out of the country, national converts will be left behind; and national believers with thousands of 'written missionaries' will continue to spread the message of God and His salvation."

In 1961, LFTL provided three million Gospel portions for Assemblies of God missionaries. Sam was elated, but knew in his heart that the best was yet to come.

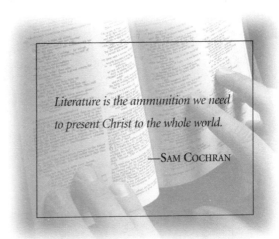

Literature is the ammunition we need to present Christ to the whole world.

—SAM COCHRAN

five
Target Cities

SAM SPENT MORE AND MORE TIME away from his business to raise funds for LFTL. He was Sunday School superintendent at Santa Ana First Assembly, head of the insurance department at Orange Coast College, and founding president of the advisory board of Southern California College in Costa Mesa.

By 1961, the Cochran household teemed with children. James was 12, Ronald was 10, Susan was 6, and Gary was 2.

Sam traveled extensively promoting LFTL. It was not unusual for him to be gone at least two weekends a month, speaking at fund-raising banquets or meeting with other LFTL supporters to plan upcoming events and promotions. Sam especially welcomed any opportunity to speak in a district that did not have an active LFTL program. If he could meet with key business people and tell about his vision and the pressing need for missions literature, chances are that district soon caught fire for LFTL. Sam's testimony was that compelling.

In 1961, LFTL joined forces with Global Conquest, the Department of Foreign Missions' extended effort to take the

Light for the Lost gospel literature was printed in a local print shop in Rome, Italy, in 1961 and distributed at the Brancaccio Theater where thousands gathered each night to hear evangelist Hal Herman and missionary Al Perna. Courtesy The Pentecostal Evangel.

gospel to the entire world, to target many of the world's largest population centers for citywide evangelistic campaigns. LFTL became the arm of the national fellowship that provided literature for campaigns in Dakar, Senegal; Taipei, Taiwan; Djakarta, Indonesia; Dacca, Pakistan; Tokyo, Japan; Montevideo, Uruguay; Tegucigalpa, Honduras; and Caracas, Venezuela.

Before each crusade, Assemblies of God missionaries trained national pastors and workers in special methods of personal evangelism. LFTL armed the workers with the printed Word of God as they fanned out to all sections of the targeted cities.

Rome, Italy, the very center of the Catholic universe, was the first target city. LFTL sent a check for $2,500 to print 100,000 Gospels of John for distribution. Evangelists Harold "Hal" Herman and Alfred J. "Al" Perna planned the campaign "with fear and trembling" because such an effort had not been attempted in Italy in more than 100 years.

ABOVE: *Members of a local Assemblies of God youth group ready to distribute evangelistic literature in Rome, Italy. Courtesy* The Pentecostal Evangel.

ABOVE (inset): *Missionary Mrs. J.W. Tucker gives Light for the Lost literature to a new convert in the Congo in Africa. Courtesy* The Pentecostal Evangel.

During the spring of 1961, God provided a 2,500 seat theater in the heart of Rome. Herman and Perna used the LFTL money to print a Gospel of John with a deep yellow and brown cover containing a picture of a stream of water gushing from a rock. The Gospel was called, "The Fountain of Living Water."

Perna remembered the two weeks of revival in July 1961, "What a thrill it was to see the theater filled every night as crowds gathered to listen to the words of life. Many were healed and many more were saved. With joy we watched the people accept a copy of the Gospel of John as they entered the theater."

Rev. U.N. Gorietti, the general superintendent of the Italian Assemblies of God, served as host pastor in the Rome meetings. He urged the congregation to carry the LFTL-provided Gospels with them and prayerfully read them every day. The results of the target campaign were evident. At the close of the revival, 1,200 persons enrolled in Bible correspondence courses. Over 1,000 people filled out convert cards. Six months later, at a Sunday

RIGHT: *The Assemblies of God Gospel Publishing House printed brochures for distribution at Light for the Lost banquets and at church services promoting the literature program for target cities.*

BELOW: *Sam served as a deacon and chairman of the finance committee at First Assembly of God in Santa Ana, California. A ribbon-cutting celebrated the dedication of the church's new sanctuary in 1962. Left to right, Sam, the Santa Ana police chief, and pastor Earl W. Odell.* Courtesy The Pentecostal Evangel.

Sam speaking to a Light for the Lost rally in southern California in 1964.
At left is missionary to Africa Morris Plotts.

night service in an Assemblies of God church in Rome, Hal Herman asked how many were present who had first heard the message during the July revival. More than 60 people raised their hands.

Another early target city for LFTL and Global Conquest was Mexico City, the capital of Mexico. The campaign in May 1962, was directed by Assemblies of God missionary Arthur Lindvall, on loan from his post in El Salvador.

Mexican Christians spent a week in prayer and fasting and dedicated themselves to literature evangelism and personal witnessing. Volunteers in groups of two went from house to house, distributed Gospel portions, and gave inquirers an opportunity to accept Christ. Those responding were asked to sign a card indicating their decision. They were called *simpatizantes*, those friendly to the gospel. The price of separation was high for new converts. Many had to give up their closest friends in the Catholic-dominated city. Some new Christians were renounced as dead by their families.

Opposition to the targeting of Mexico City was great. However, as the campaign progressed, the Holy Spirit opened hearts and area churches began to grow. Within a few months most Assemblies of God churches reported at least a doubling in size. Five particular churches and their 16 branch Sunday Schools increased 400 percent by the time Sam arrived in late August to film the results of the target campaign.

Sam was in awe of God's move. He wrote in *The Pentecostal Evangel*, "As I attended 'victory rallies,' I realized that the Mexican Christians were deeply dedicated to the Lord. My fellowship with them and their executive brethren was an experience I will never forget. Then it dawned on me. This soul-winning campaign was not closing…it was just beginning!" It was no surprise to Sam when missionaries asked him for 100,000 more copies of Gospel portions for a renewed house-to-house effort in Mexico City.

The urgency of the need for literature for use in the target cities was expressed by National Men's Fellowship Secretary Burton W. Pierce in *The Pentecostal Evangel*. Pierce wrote, "LFTL is a businessman's approach to accelerating the harvest in these final days before Jesus comes. Every cent given for overseas soul winning goes for that purpose. There are no deductions for expenses. Such expenses are underwritten through Men's Fellowship by key laymen who are interested in doing business for God in the most economical way. We invite every man to invest his dollars wisely, accompanied by united intercessory prayer for a move of the Holy Spirit in an unusual way. For perhaps, this will be the final great harvest in these major cities of the earth."

Thousands of converts were reported by Hal Herman in a 1963 revival campaign in Managua, Nicaragua. Herman gave much of the credit to LFTL, writing, "Souls are being won to Christ and countless lives changed today through the worldwide

RIGHT: *Young people prepare to distribute Light for the Lost literature to the unsaved of Managua, Nicaragua, in 1963. Courtesy* The Pentecostal Evangel.

ABOVE: *Left to right, Evangelist Hal Herman, Missionary Russell Kensinger, and Nicaraguan Pastor Juan Videa examine Light for the Lost literature distributed to the thousands who attended nightly crusades in Managua, Nicaragua. Courtesy* The Pentecostal Evangel.

literature outreach." He called LFTL "a wonderful channel through which Christian men can have a personal and direct influence in reaching multitudes of lost souls with the message of Jesus Christ."

LFTL spread to other districts of the Assemblies of God. In 1963, laymen in New Jersey pledged $400 to provide 88,000 Gospel portions for distribution in Tegucigalpa, Honduras. The

A great crowd in Africa rejoices at receiving copies of the Gospel of John printed in their language. Light for the Lost funds were used to design and print the Gospel portion.

give me the book!

pledge came after Dr. Jere D. Melilli, a Baton Rouge, Louisiana, surgeon presented the challenge of soul winning to more than 400 New Jersey men and boys at a "Lads and Dads" banquet.

During May 1963, a new record of $3,326.89 for monthly nationwide giving was established, led by the Southern California District with an offering of $1,820.00. Men in Southern California began cooking steaks for local Light for the Lost banquets. The profits went directly to LFTL. It was estimated that the contributions in that one month would provide nearly 700,000 Gospel portions and a much larger quantity of evangelistic tracts. More than 40 foreign cities were scheduled for major literature crusades in 1963.

In South Africa, Missionaries E.E. Shaffer and John Richards loaded their tents and boxes of LFTL literature and headed into Bechuanaland, an area that had been closed for years to the gospel. Shaffer remembered, "On the second night an African political party staged a demonstration, marching belligerently around the tent while singing political songs. But again the meeting was a huge success. Several hundred people responded to the gospel invitation, and many of them experienced genuine conversions."

Thousands of pieces of LFTL literature were distributed in advance of Shaffer and Richards' tent campaign that saw people come from distant villages to hear the gospel. Shaffer wrote, "How thankful we are to Men's Fellowship for their contribution of LFTL literature."

A half million pieces of literature were distributed to almost every household in Kuala Lumpur, Malaysia. Praying Christians stuffed each of 100,000 clear plastic envelopes with two tracts in English, two in Chinese, and a self-addressed postcard. The bright red and blue tracts made a most attractive packet. Missionary Delmar Guynes reported that 60,000 families were reached and 1,200 requests for additional literature were received. A LFTL evangelistic crusade, led by Loren Cunningham, climaxed the literature crusade in Kuala Lumpur. Every night people came forward for salvation, people who had been reached by the advance literature distribution.

LFTL provided $1,000 to print 100,000 copies of a miniature Bible in Portuguese for Revivaltime Evangelist C.M. Ward's 1963 campaign in Brazil. Walter Hanson, a Sacramento, California businessman whom Sam had encouraged to enter LFTL, accompanied Ward. Hanson reported, "At the conclusion of each service the brethren gathered, together with Brother Ward and me, and took the boxes containing several thousand of the little miniature Bibles and tracts and placed their hands upon them and prayed that the Lord would use each one as it was handed out. The people could not wait and came running to the platform with hands outstretched, their eyes pleading, 'Give me one please.'"

Minnesota District LFTL councilmen pledged $3,000 for a 1963 literature campaign in Lagos, the capital of Nigeria. Missionary Robert Webb wrote, "Due to the urgency of the need, the money has been advanced, and we are now implementing literature distribution as well as using the literature for Bible study courses. Through these Bible courses we believe the effectiveness of this literature program will be far-reaching indeed."

In British Guiana, LFTL provided funds to print 50,000 copies of an eight-page magazine. Missionary Paul Palser reported thrilling results. In one town, a young high school student, the only Protestant in a Moslem and Catholic home, so desired to share his joy in Christ with fellow students that he and his friends distributed 4,500 copies of the magazine to high school students.

In March 1963, during the national Men's Fellowship seminar, Glen Bonds, a layman who owned a wholesale produce business in Pomona, California, was appointed executive vice president of the National LFTL Council. Bonds was charged with promoting LFTL in rallies and church services in Southern California and adjoining districts.

In August 1963, Operation Saturation was launched in Japan. Missionary Paul Klahr supervised the placing of ads in newspapers and distribution of LFTL literature. In Osaka, evangelist Louis Hauff conducted a campaign following the LFTL rally. Hundreds were saved and 900 people signed up for a Bible correspondence course.

The Ralph Byrd evangelistic team held meetings in Seoul, Masan, and Chongu, South Korea. More than 500,000 tracts, 20,000 Gospel portions, 1,000 Bibles, and 40,000 copies of the Korean *Evangel* were distributed. Missionary John Hurston reported, "The zeal of Pentecostal youth to witness and distribute literature is having a great influence throughout Korea. Crowds attending meetings ranged from 2,000 in the smaller cities to 4,000 in Seoul." LFTL sent $1,000 for the Korean literature campaign. Within weeks, a request was made for another $1,200, a request filled in faith by the national LFTL office.

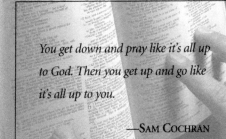

You get down and pray like it's all up to God. Then you get up and go like it's all up to you.

—SAM COCHRAN

six

A Transferable Vision

SINCE JESUS GAVE THE GREAT COMMISSION, "Go ye into all the world, and preach the gospel," there have been thousands of good ideas on how to reach the lost. Some have been successful; most have not. What made the difference in Sam's vision to take the written Word to all peoples of the earth? Many of Sam's converts to the mission of LFTL over the past four decades agree that Sam's ability to "transfer the vision" to others was what enabled LFTL to bridge the wide chasm from idea to successful fruition.

Ray Neill, who had been introduced to LFTL by original MGS supporter Lloyd Waterfield, enthusiastically joined LFTL in 1959 because he saw Sam as "a man of action." Sam's vision was transferred to Neill because he believed that the idea of using laymen to assist missionaries in the field was "God-given." Neill recalled, "LFTL was an immediate fit for me." Neill became Sam's constant companion at rallies and banquets for decades to come.

By 1962, four years into the program at the national level, Sam had enrolled only 13 new councilmen to help with monthly administrative expenses. He asked God to provide some creative way to spread the interest in LFTL to Assemblies of God men across the nation. God clearly directed Sam to plan a series of banquets in which men and their wives would be enticed to attend, to have a nice meal, and hear about the urgent need to take the Word to the lost masses of the world.

Ray Neill had workers at his Long Beach, California, aircraft plant build sheet metal barbecue wagons that councilmen could use to cook steaks for banquets at local churches throughout southern California. Sam wanted to make it easy for pastors to say "yes" to his request to hold a LFTL banquet. If the pastor knew the food was taken care of, he might be more likely to allow the event.

Twenty-five-year-old Robert "Bob" Bruder was invited to a LFTL rally in Los Angeles in 1963 by Judge Lindsay, his pastor at Covina, California, Assembly of God. Actually, Lindsay "twisted" Bruder's arm to get him to attend the meeting at which Sam and Assemblies of God Pastor Otis Keener shared the LFTL message. Bruder was drawn to LFTL by Sam's absolute dedication and his "overwhelming charisma."

Bruder remembered, "With only about 100 men actively supporting the project, Sam was desperate to add councilmen and increase the commitment of existing councilmen to the cause. Sam often quoted D.L. Moody who said, 'Show me your check book and I will determine your commitment.'" Bruder immediately caught Sam's vision for LFTL and used his private airplane to fly to rallies and banquets. He traveled with Sam on early tours in southern California and surrounding states. "Sam was so tight with administrative funds," Bruder recalled, "we always stayed in one room at a Motel 6."

Sam's persistence paid off. Many times he was able to convince a pastor to give him the Sunday morning service by calling with

Sam worked hard to transfer his vision to send the Word of God to evangelize the whole world. He would not take "no" for an answer. If a pastor at first refused to entertain his request for a service, he called until the pastor gave in.

the bold statement, "I have a vision I need to share with your people. I'll be there at 10:30 this morning."

Pastor Ralph Hilton had established a new church, Glad Tidings Assembly of God, in Tucson, Arizona, only a few months before Sam called. Hilton, who never knew how Sam knew to call him, remembered, "Sam said he was going to be in Arizona on insurance business and just wanted to share his vision." With only 35 people in attendance at the new church, Sam told about LFTL and his burning desire to raise money to send literature for Assemblies of God missionaries to use in evangelism. Hilton said, "From that date, Sam's vision was transferred to me. It caught fire and changed me. I know Sam's vision had to come from the very heart of God."

Men who experienced the transfer of Sam's vision to their own soul launched out across the country to bring more men into the battle to provide missionaries with much-needed literature. Phil Brauchler was working in his aircraft business in Fort Lauderdale,

Pastor Ralph Hilton met Sam Cochran on the telephone. Sam was asking for a service to tell the story of Light for the Lost. Courtesy Robert Burke.

Florida, one day when a stranger drove up in a pickup truck pulling a camper trailer. The stranger was Glen Bonds who had caught Sam's vision and had gone to work to add more councilmen and increase giving for the missions literature fund.

Bonds told Brauchler, "I was sent by 'Pappy' Bush to sign you up for Light for the Lost." Brauchler, as a member of Bethel First Assembly of God in Fort Lauderdale knew Bush as a national pro-

give me the book!

Phil Brauchler saw the great hunger for literature on a trip to help distribute literature with his brother, Missionary David Brauchler, in Bogota, Colombia. Instructions given to novice literature distributors were simple, "Move fast and don't run out! The people will either get a piece of literature, a piece of your shirt, or a piece of your hide." On one particular afternoon in Bogota, Brauchler exhausted his supply of literature and was forced to back into a building to get away from the converging crowd, all hungry for the written Word. Courtesy Robert Burke.

moter of Assemblies of God missions but thought Bonds was talking about some program for the blind. Bonds explained LFTL and the need for councilmen. Brauchler said he did not have time and $15 a month councilman dues would strain his budget.

Bonds, taking the trait of persistency from Sam, his LFTL mentor, told Brauchler, "That's OK. I have a camper outside.

Men attending the Light for the Lost banquet in El Dorado, Arkansas, listen intently to the missionary challenge. Courtesy The Pentecostal Evangel.

RIGHT: *Victory smiles abound at a Light for the Lost banquet in Fresno, California. Left to right, master of ceremonies Paul Evans, speaker Wesley Hurst, Glen Bonds, Floyd Waterfield, and Sam. Courtesy* The Pentecostal Evangel.

BELOW: *A Light for the Lost literature team in Bombay, India, ready to distribute 250,000 tracts. Courtesy* The Pentecostal Evangel.

RIGHT: *Tons of Light for the Lost literature is readied for distribution in South America. Courtesy The Pentecostal Evangel.*

LEFT: *Men of the Southern California District provided funds in 1964 to distribute Light for the Lost literature in Formosa. This gospel wagon was used to carry LFTL literature and advertise tent meetings. Courtesy The Pentecostal Evangel.*

The map shows nine major areas in Africa for Light for the Lost literature saturation programs. Left to right, Russell Cox, Arizona District Men's Fellowship Director; Arizona LFTL banquet speaker Howard S. Bush; and Sam. Courtesy **The Pentecostal Evangel.**

'Pappy' told me to stay until I have you signed up.'" Brauchler signed a councilman card and paid his first $15. He remembered, "From that moment, God blessed my business in incredible ways. Never did I have to worry about paying the monthly dues."

Brauchler's heart was touched by the infant work of LFTL. He began speaking to potential councilmen on tours in Florida and adjoining states. He and Sam became "soul mates" in taking the LFTL message to Assemblies of God men everywhere.

Men attending the 10th anniversary LFTL banquet in Los Angeles in 1963 pledged $22,000. Sam and Howard Bush addressed the banquet, reporting on victory rallies in Japan.

Another $5,000 was raised at a banquet in Fresno, California, where Wesley R. Hurst was the principal speaker.

Arkansas joined the list of LFTL districts in August, 1963, when laymen and pastors of churches in and around El Dorado conducted a LFTL banquet meeting at First Assembly in El Dorado. More than $1,000 was pledged to provide gospel literature for a major evangelistic effort in Bombay, India. More than 250,000 tracts and leaflets were printed. Missionary James Anderson preached to more than a thousand people each night. He wrote, "The results were far beyond expectation for a non-Christian community such as this. Among the converts were college students, factory workers, a lawyer, and many other people representing all walks of life."

In 1964, Arizona men, in their first district-wide LFTL banquet, pledged $8,000 for literature for evangelism in nine strategic cities in Africa. Howard S. Bush was the featured speaker for the banquet.

Other districts began holding annual LFTL banquets. By the spring of 1964, nearly $70,000 was pledged in the previous 11 months to evangelize cities in the Far East, Near East, Europe, Latin America, and Africa.

> *For the first time in our history, we are able to build a total evangelism force.*
>
> —J. PHILIP HOGAN

seven

Calcutta and Beyond

"THIS IS THE HOUR! TOMORROW WILL BE TOO LATE! This is the hour when we must put the precious Word of God into the hands of these eternity-bound multitudes." Those words by Assemblies of God Missionary Mark Buntain highlighted his plea in 1965 for increased LFTL funds to evangelize Calcutta, India, a city of seven million people crammed into 36 square miles.

Buntain was already printing 90,000 tracts per month, each stamped with the invitation for the reader to enroll in his Bible correspondence school. However, Buntain wanted to do more. He described the need, "The thing that points daggers at Christian visitors in India is the throngs of people, millions of souls moving like human ants, slowly shuffling along the highway of life. I have seen our Assemblies of God visitors break down and weep at the sight of millions of people. One of our lady evangelists could not

BELOW: *Planning a Light for Lost blitz on South America are, left to right, Sam, Evangelist Wesley Hurst, and LFTL National President Glen Bonds.*

LEFT: *At General Council in 1965, First Assembly of God in Binghamton, New York, was honored for giving the most offerings to Light for the Lost. Pastor R.D.E. Smith, center, was awarded a trophy by Everett James, left, and Howard Bush, a frequent speaker for LFTL banquets. Courtesy The Pentecostal Evangel.*

RIGHT: *Sam was featured on the cover of Team, a monthly publication of the Assemblies of God Men's Fellowship Department in August 1965. The cover promoted Sam's speech to the Men's Fellowship breakfast during General Council in Des Moines, Iowa.*

BELOW: *Arm in arm at a southern California hotel are, left to right, Dr. Robert Schuller, pastor of the Crystal Cathedral in Garden Grove, California; Colonel Harlan Sanders, founder of Kentucky Fried Chicken; and Sam.*

calcutta and beyond

leave her room for four days, she was so overwhelmed at the sight of the Christless crowd."

Buntain coordinated LFTL rallies with the West Bengal Bible Correspondence School. In October 1965, Buntain conducted "the greatest gospel literature crusade ever attempted" in that part of the world. Thousands of students, armed with tracts and Gospels provided by LFTL, went into the streets of Calcutta and into the state of West Bengal with a population of 40 million people. Buntain said, "Thank God, we have the young people to do the job. What we must have now is the printed material, the ammunition to place in the hands of these young people."

In the Dum Dum crusade, in an area around the Calcutta airport, 125,000 plastic bags with LFTL tracts and booklets were handed out to people living in cardboard boxes and shacks. Buntain, who became a legend in Calcutta, expressed his appreciation to Assemblies of God laymen. He wrote, "All of this evangelistic fervor could never have been accomplished without the tremendous help from LFTL. We here at the crossroads of the East can only thank God from the bottom of our hearts for every Assemblies of God layman who is making this great literature program possible."

The year 1965 was a banner year for LFTL efforts worldwide. Tommy Barnett asked for special literature for a nine-night crusade in the Victoria Theatre in Singapore. Publications called *Bookmarks* were designed to attract the attention of the youth of Singapore.

In Ecuador, the newest mission field of the Assemblies of God, LFTL joined hands with missionaries in a pioneer effort. Missionary Lowell Dowdy wrote, "Saturday we went to a market to hand out tracts and gospels. The people made a rush for the literature…our fellows had to run for their lives, they were being smothered! We had two growing Pentecostal works in less than five months of services."

May 2, 1965, was promoted as Light for the Lost Sunday at Assemblies of God churches nationwide. In sending out envelopes for offerings to the more than 9,000 Assemblies of God churches, National Field Secretary Everett James wrote, "LFTL is not scattering seed. It is planting a garden. Each piece of literature is placed in the hands of a genuinely interested person. Assemblies of God laymen are reaching around the world!"

Laymen of the Northern California-Nevada District committed $20,500 for LFTL literature to be used in a year-long campaign in Nigeria. Good News Crusades were planned for the major cities in Nigeria.

In Costa Rica, national pastors met for months in advance of a major evangelistic effort. Missionary John Bueno left his post in El Salvador to preach crusades in San Jose. Missionary David Godwin told about the campaign, "We taught our people about the value of literature. Each church sent its teams to the front lines for house-to-house visitation. For the first time many believers saw a real hunger for the gospel among their fellow citizens." Costa Rican Christians handed out thousands of copies of *Poder*, the Spanish equivalent of *The Pentecostal Evangel*.

In 1966, in advance of observation of National LFTL Day on the first Sunday in May, Missionary to Korea Louis Richards wrote in *The Evangel*:

> What does Light for the Lost do? I will tell you. Because of Light for the Lost, the effectiveness of our missionaries has been multiplied many times. Take our field, Korea, for example. Hundreds of thousands of salvation tracts and other pieces of gospel literature have been distributed here in the past year. Our mission in Pusan has, for the past 12 years, supplied tracts and full-gospel literature to ministers and layworkers throughout the entire province, because laymen in the U.S. have caught the vision of what can be done. When your church observes Light for the Lost Day on May 1, I hope you will give generously. God is blessing this literature outreach throughout the world.

Eager hands reach for literature supplied by Light for the Lost during a Paul Olson Good News Crusade in Sierra Leone in Africa. Courtesy The Pentecostal Evangel.

First Assembly of God in Redlands, California, was the top-giving church to LFTL in 1966. The church's pastor, Lloyd Reece, said, "We are only doing a small part to carry the gospel of Jesus to our neighbors all over the world."

Evangelist Paul Olson took LFTL literature to the small West African country of Sierra Leone in 1967. The Good News Crusade was a joint effort of LFTL and Global Conquest. In five weeks, over 4,000 Africans turned from heathenism to worship Jesus Christ. Five thousand copies of a message entitled *The Mark of a Christian* were distributed at the close of the campaign. *The Evangel's* foreign missions editor, David Womack, wrote, "The

story never got into the world's newspapers or on television newscasts, but it must have been recorded very carefully in the books of heaven."

The presses kept rolling to supply missionaries with much needed literature. South Pacific Missionary Lawrence R. Larson wrote, "Ministers in Fiji are convinced that evangelistic literature,

BELOW: *Oklahoma's Chuck Freeman addresses a Light for the Lost banquet. Freeman's story is typical of laymen who became part of Sam's vision. Freeman began to donate his time to LFTL and God blessed his business.*

printed in their own language, will help them reach souls and build a strong church. Often LFTL tracts just off the press are in the hands of needy souls before the ink is dry! When we send a shipment of 10,000 tracts to the Tongan Islands, the believers distribute them immediately. To keep these Christian workers busy, a tract distribution will require a steadier and more plentiful supply."

To provide the steadier and more plentiful supply of literature meant raising more money. Sam and the national office of LFTL stepped up their efforts to gain acceptance in more districts of the Assemblies of God and adding more LFTL councilmen to bear the administrative burden.

In 1966, Charles "Chuck" Freeman, who had become a councilman several years before, introduced LFTL to Oklahoma District Superintendent Robert Goggin, who contributed the first $600. Through a series of sectional meetings, Freeman and James Holt of Tulsa took the LFTL message throughout Oklahoma. Holt's church, Woodlake Assembly of God in Tulsa, was the second church in the nation to have 100 councilmen. The first church to reach that lofty plateau was First Assembly of God in Des Moines, Iowa.

Freeman became famous throughout the Southwest for cooking ribs for LFTL banquets and retreats. He used the ribs to get into Oklahoma churches. He saw a cooker for sale and thought if he could buy it, he could cook steaks and ribs for men and then present the LFTL program to them. The response was unbelievable. Freeman, along with Sam, was also responsible for taking the LFTL message to districts in Texas.

Glen Bonds, national secretary of the Men's Fellowship Department, and one of the first LFTL councilmen, set a goal of $10,000 in offerings for the 1967 National LFTL Day. The emphasis of the appeal was revival crusades planned for Bombay, India. Bonds said, "We have picked Bombay because it is the seventh largest city in the world. Because its seaport draws workers from all over India, the effects of our evangelism there will reach thousands in many other towns and villages." More than two million pieces of literature were handed out in Bombay. Replies requesting more literature were received from 75,000 Indians.

Reports of great revivals assisted by the distribution of LFTL literature streamed into the national office. From Bolivia, Tonga, France, Peru, Switzerland, and India came reports of thousands of people saved from eternal damnation because of the introduction to Christ through an inexpensive piece of gospel literature.

In Monrovia, Liberia, 135,000 tracts were distributed prior to a crusade held by Evangelist Paul Olson. More than a half million pieces of literature were handed out in Paris, France, before a Hal Herman crusade. Major cities in Bolivia were literally saturated with gospel literature provided by LFTL.

By 1968, it was estimated that LFTL had paid for the printing of over 30 million pieces of literature for Assemblies of God missions efforts. Foreign Missions Executive Director J. Philip Hogan said, "For the first time in our history, we are able to build a total evangelism force. First are the missionaries. Then, there are evangelists who are turning toward the foreign field. Finally, there is Light for the Lost to provide literature. Nothing that has happened on the mission field has gladdened the hearts of missionaries any more than LFTL. Our 918 Assemblies of God missionaries working in 78 countries are rejoicing over the results of this effective way of reaching the lost."

Singapore was again targeted for evangelization in 1968. All monies raised on National Light for the Lost Day were earmarked to provide literature for a renewed effort to take the gospel to the city of nearly two million people. LFTL made available a copy of the Book of Acts and the Gospel of John for each new convert, together with a Scripture memorization guide and a card to enroll in a correspondence course.

Assemblies of God believers throughout Argentina, supplied with over 725,000 pieces of LFTL literature, reached 50,000 homes with the message of salvation. Hundreds of conversions were reported. One young man sent a copy of *Words of Life* to a relative in a distant province. The relative wrote back that he had accepted Christ only because of being introduced to the Savior by LFTL literature. The booklet had traveled over a thousand kilometers and had found a receptive heart.

The value of literature in Good News Crusades was expressed by missionary Harold Carpenter and Evangelist Hugh Jeter after a revival in Bolivia. Carpenter said, "As I hear the reports of souls saved in each campaign, I say thanks to God for LFTL and for the fruit that remains as a result of its literature used in Good News Crusades."

The 1969 Light for the Lost Sunday target city was Kinshasa, capital of what was then called Congo in Africa. LFTL literature designed by local artists was distributed to thousands of homes.

Also in 1969, Paul Crouch, now president of the Trinity Broadcasting Network (TBN), and Sam flew to Singapore to film footage for a new LFTL film, Good News in Singapore.

By the end of the 1960s, LFTL was a major force in world missions for the Assemblies of God. Annual contributions had risen from $392 in 1953; to $31,901 in 1963; to $137,182 in 1967, and to an incredible $218,352 in 1969. Another $40,000 was raised in 1969 to operate the national LFTL office.

In 1969, the Assembly of God in Holland, Michigan, was the top church in giving to LFTL, with offerings of $6,225. Second on the list was First Assembly in Phoenix, Arizona, followed by First Assembly in Van Buren, Arkansas; the Assembly of God in Covina, California; Bethel Assembly in San Jose, California; First Assembly in Wilmington, California; Bethel Temple in Dayton, Ohio; First Assembly in Visalia, California; Fair Ridge Assembly in Shade Gap, Pennsylvania; and the Assembly of God in Redlands, California. Thirty five churches gave more than $1,000 in 1969.

Southern California had the most churches giving, 126. Oklahoma was second, with 111 churches sending a LFTL offering to Springfield. In all, churches in 50 Assemblies of God districts contributed to LFTL.

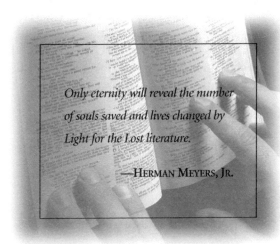

Only eternity will reveal the number of souls saved and lives changed by Light for the Lost literature.

—HERMAN MEYERS, JR.

eight
Motivational Speaker

IN ADDITION TO SPENDING MUCH OF HIS TIME and effort building LFTL across the nation, Sam's business interests expanded. He founded and managed Local Insurance Service, Inc., Advanced Insurance Marketing, Inc., and Risk Consultants, Inc., all southern California insurance concerns. He received lifetime insurance teaching credentials from the State of California, a PhD in Commercial Science from London University's Institute for Applied Research, and a BS in Business Administration, Master of Arts in Business, and PhD in Insurance and Risk Management from the Calgary College of Technology in Calgary, Alberta, Canada.

Sam wrote articles for trade publications on leadership development and management. He developed a tape and worksheet series on business management and ethics. He was invited to address both business and church groups.

"How to be a leader" was the subject of a speech that Sam gave to hundreds of groups. In the speech, he listed ten points that, in his opinion, governed personal power:

The habit of definiteness of purpose
Promptness of decision
Soundness of character
Strict discipline over one's emotions
Obsessional desire to render useful service
Thorough knowledge of your subject
Tolerance on all subjects
Loyalty to one's personal associates
Enduring thirst for knowledge
Alertness of imagination

In his motivational leadership seminars, Sam emphasized the traits of a leader, the habit of smiling, tactfulness, manners and speech, the need for a keen sense of humor and justice, faithfulness, emotional control, and a genuine fondness for people.

Sam enjoyed talking to people about Sunday School. He was a strong believer in distinct departmentalization of Sunday School, from sleepers and creepers to adult Bible classes. He thought the key to solid growth was departmentalization. He wrote, "Through it, more control can be brought about, control necessary to be sure the student is receiving the proper teaching. Since teaching is not an exact science, careful control is accomplished through small units where departmental superintendents are very close to the teachers who are able to detect problems immediately. Any weakness of the teacher or inconsistency is discovered before great damage is done."

In his talks to Sunday School superintendents and teachers, Sam preached practical ideas like, "Be sure your rest room facilities are as close to the very young age children as possible so as not to create a disturbance during class time."

The story of Sam's vision which resulted in the establishment of Light for the Lost was featured in the summer 1970 edition of Real Living, *a publication of the National Men's Fellowship Department of the Canadian Assemblies of God.*

In the late 1960s, Sam's title in the LFTL program was changed from national coordinator to national president. At the 1970 LFTL national convention in Springfield, he reported that he had spoken at 17 LFTL rallies or services the previous year and that Northwest, Ohio, Minnesota, Michigan, and North Texas had been added to the growing list of active LFTL districts.

By 1970, 300 LFTL councilmen contributed $15 monthly to pay administrative costs. National Vice-Chairman Herman Meyer, Jr., expressed to convention delegates the need for an even greater effort, saying, "From every continent have come requests for more literature than ever before as our missionaries repeatedly inform us that this printed material is the vital tool that aids them in the task of reaching and ministering unto the multitudes of lost souls in their areas...Only eternity will reveal the number of souls saved and lives that were changed as people accepted Christ for the first time."

LFTL Secretary Everett James set out to build a stronger relationship between LFTL leaders and Men's Fellowship leaders in each of the districts of the Assemblies of God. James urged LFTL units to meet several times a year.

Evangelist Bernhard Johnson held Good News Crusades throughout the world, especially in Brazil, where the Assemblies of God registered millions of new adherents beginning in the 1970s. Light for the Lost printed material was an integral part of Johnson's efforts.

Evangelist Willard Cantelon assisted the Northern California-Nevada District in raising nearly $50,000 in 1970. At the annual Men's Fellowship banquet in Oakland, California, 1,000 people saw LFTL committee members put on a skit. A GMC van loaded with literature was driven to the center of the stage. Then several men came forward and unloaded literature, distributing the new LFTL brochure to everyone in attendance.

LFTL developed a list of excellent speakers to take the message to banquets and rallies. Everett James and Glen Bonds made the banquet circuit in Washington and Oregon. Bill Wind and Don Pittman led efforts in Arizona. Lloyd Waterfield built a booth for LFTL that was used at special missionary meetings and services in southern California. Ellis Damiani was recognized for his work in Ohio.

In 1970, six executive vice presidents provided leadership for LFTL in different regions of the country. They were Eugene K. Roe, Northwest; Robert G. Bruder, Southwest; Charles R. Turner, North Central; Chuck Freeman, South Central; John T. Tyler, Great Lakes; and Julius L. Fried, Northeast.

Bruder chaired a five-year advance planning committee. Other members included Duane Anderson, John Bachman, Stanley Benjamin, Clark Blackinton, Monte Brown, Doyle Burgess, Thomas Castleberry, Gerald Cooley, Robert Englander, Ed Freeburg, Darrell Herman, Steven Kish, David Klein, Donald

Sam, left, speaks through an interpreter at a rally in Tokyo, Japan. The rally launched an Operation Saturation tour in which Light for the Lost literature was used to saturate entire sections of the sprawling Japanese city.

Sam presents a pledge poster to a Light for the Lost councilman at a 1971 banquet.

Kolstad, Daniel Lubelan, Lee Mindt, Ray Radford, James Stoutemyer, Allen Walters, and Warren Wheat.

Eight veteran LFTL councilmen served on the nominations committee, chaired by Hollis Lawson. Members of the committee were Delmer Cramer, Morris Hendrickson, Sam Ohler, Eugene Roe, Earl Seward, and Robert Thompson.

Sam chaired the resolutions committee for the 1970 national convention. Members of the committee were Robert Vickers, Lloyd Waterfield, Chester Roberts, Norman Underwood, G.F. Scoggin, Glen Norwood, Merlyn Muench, and Lester Hughes.

In 1971, LFTL passed the $1 million mark in accumulative total giving since 1953. Foreign Missions Director J. Philip Hogan gave LFTL much of the credit in opening new mission fields in Ecuador, Rhodesia, Panama, New Hebrides, Ivory Coast, Tonga,

g i v e   m e   t h e   b o o k !

and Thailand. Hogan said, "To mention the cities reached just this past year would sound like a world geography lesson."

The Foreign Missions Board appointed Everett James in 1971 as an overseas literature coordinator. His duties included training national leaders in methods of Christian witnessing, literature distribution, and related ministries. James had faithfully served LFTL and its predecessor organizations for 18 years. He was replaced as national LFTL secretary by Ellis Damiani, an Ohio pastor who had caught the vision for LFTL.

Once again Sam's title changed in 1971. He became national chairman of the LFTL Executive Committee. Herman Meyer, Jr., was national vice-chairman and Phil Sondeno, a contractor from Northern California, was national president. Richard Patete, a Cleveland, Ohio, banker, was the new regional executive vice president in the Great Lakes Region, Hollis Lawson served in the same position in the Gulf Region, and Phil Brachler was the regional executive vice president in the Southeast Region.

Services at the 1971 national convention at the Disneyland Hotel

Mark Buntain, missionary to Calcutta, India, preaches to a Light for the Lost banquet in southern California in 1972. At his left is National LFTL Secretary Ellis Damiani.

Bill Davis, right, with Southern California District Superintendent Ray Rachels at the 2001 national Light for the Lost convention. Courtesy Robert Burke.

in Anaheim, California, were broadcast live over KHOF FM, managed by Paul Crouch. Crouch enthusiastically supported LFTL and spearheaded efforts to develop LFTL missions films.

Assemblies of God General Superintendent Thomas F. Zimmerman was the keynote convention speaker in 1971. A new program, the Gold Key Club, was introduced to reward councilmen who aggressively signed up new LFTL councilmen.

Sam spoke to a group of men at First Assembly of God in La Mesa, California, in 1971. In the audience was Bill Davis. He remembered, "Sam was so intense. The Holy Spirit clearly told me to become a councilman and begin actively helping Sam to carry the burden of raising money for LFTL." Sam accepted

Davis's offer of help and put him to work on tours in southern California. According to Davis, "I had sat on a church pew for years and heard many programs presented. But, somehow, Sam's message was different. His vision became my vision. From the first night I heard about LFTL, I wanted to be an active part of it."

LFTL continued to choose a target city each year on which to focus fund-raising activities on the first Sunday in May. In 1971 both LFTL and Good News Crusades descended upon Calcutta to help Missionary Mark Buntain and other Assemblies of God workers reach a forgotten people. Young people went out in teams to distribute hundreds of thousands of LFTL tracts and booklets. The material was paid for by LFTL but printed in Calcutta in the technical department of a high school Buntain operated.

Buntain was thankful for LFTL attention to his city. "Big people and big businesses have forsaken Calcutta," he wrote, "God still looks down with tender pity and outstretched arms to all of His inhabitants." Calcutta had grown by two million inhabitants since LFTL targeted the city less than a decade before.

A pamphlet entitled "Christ Is the Answer" was used in many places in the world. From Tanzania, Missionary Charles Petroskey wrote, "The literature from the enemy's side is flowing thick and fast, with deadly propaganda. We must flood the area with 'Christ Is the Answer.'" J. Roland Jones, missionary to Rhodesia, reported, "The gospel in printed form has a powerful influence here. I found a man with a tract. He read the message and said he wanted to know more. He brought his brother to me. And just like in Bible times, he invited me to his home to preach. Today, that meeting has resulted in the nucleus of a church in the area. All because of one little tract."

Over 70,000 pieces of literature were distributed to people in Dahomey, in Africa. Scores of testimonies were received as a result of the International Correspondence Institute (ICI) course made possible through LFTL. Nearly 200,000 tracts were distributed in Manila, the Philippines, during Pope Paul's visit to the city.

In 1971, 462 LFTL councilmen raised sufficient money to operate the national office and spent $362,958 on literature. LFTL had become one of the great success stories of modern missions.

In Central Africa, Missionary Delmar Kingsriter thanked LFTL for more than just material. He wrote, "Not only does LFTL help us in producing tracts, but all over the countryside you can see colorful posters bearing gospel messages and advertising the crusades…all provided by LFTL. We thank God for you."

"Literature saturation evangelism" is a term coined by Foreign Missions Executive Director J. Philip Hogan in 1972. In an editorial in *The Pentecostal Evangel*, Hogan wrote:

> Light for the Lost enables a single missionary to get the good news to the masses. This has a widespread impact on many people. Through literature saturation evangelism the missionary is much more than a mere presence in a great mass of people. He is armed with a mighty proclamation, the good news that Jesus saves. He is not just one lonely witness wandering about in search of an opportunity. His ministry is multiplied thousands of times by LFTL literature.

In 1972, Saigon, Vietnam, was the target city for National Light for the Lost Day. The city of 1.5 million people had known nothing but the horrors of war since the early 1960s. Because of the great spiritual need, LFTL officials accepted the challenge to "invade" Saigon with the good news of Christ.

At the 1972 National LFTL Convention in Springfield, Sam accepted an assignment as national vice-chairman. Ray Radford, Tim Tyler, Charles Turner, Chuck Freeman, Richard Patete, Hollis

Lawson, Julius Fried, and Phil Brauchler were either retained or elected to serve as regional officers. Phil Sondeno continued as national chairman.

Also in 1972, Sam developed a presentation for LFTL leaders who were asking, "How do we put on a successful fund-raising banquet?" Sam did not recommend movies for rallies or statewide functions. Instead, he suggested sectional banquets with local pastors hosting the function. He wrote, "Should be a banquet, not a potluck. Steak dinner will bring them out; get the Women's Missionary Council involved. Decorate tables, flowers, etc. Create a good atmosphere; get the councilmen and local pastor enthused. When a section gets too big, split the section. The councilmen team should barbecue the meat. The women can prepare the rest of the meal, including the dessert." They were practical but useful hints.

At the 1972 convention, the Assembly of God in Holland, Michigan, was again named as Church-of-the-Year for raising $47,962 for LFTL. In second place for 1971 giving was First Assembly in Los Gatos, California, followed by First Assembly in Phoenix, Arizona, and the Assembly of God in Covina, California. The National LFTL Pastor-of-the-Year Award went to H. Syvelle Phillips of First Assembly in Santa Ana, California. The Southern California District led all districts by raising $84,416. Alfred Nelson of Santa Ana received the Councilman-of-the-Year Award for enlisting the most new councilmen.

Everett James and Paul Crouch co-chaired a special committee in 1972 to draft a new approach for promotional materials for LFTL. The committee suggested a cartoon-style format to describe the history of LFTL, a testimony of a councilman's involvement, a testimony of the program's effectiveness on the foreign mission fields, and specific instructions on how any man could become a councilman.

One of the most encouraging steps taken by the Assemblies of God Foreign Missions Department in the early 1970s was the establishment of modern presses in West Africa, South Africa, and East Africa. LFTL funds provided paper to print literature on modern, high-speed presses. The Assemblies of God Literature Center in Accra, Ghana, provided evangelism literature used in the countries of West Africa, including Nigeria, in which the Assemblies of God had a powerful presence. Gerald Falley, missionary and literature coordinator for West Africa, said, "It would be virtually impossible for the press to operate if it were not for LFTL."

BELOW: *Light for the Lost councilmen from First Assembly of God in Blue Springs, Missouri, prepare 300 pounds of steak for a Southern Missouri District LFTL banquet.*

Everett James continued to travel the globe to train nationals to conduct effective literature distribution programs. He said, "Literature alone can never evangelize! It requires dedicated people; a prayerfully thought-out program, and specially designed literature to do the job!"

ABOVE: *Jerry Terry came on board as a LFTL councilman in 1972. He attended Ray Neill's church in Wilmington, California. Neill handed Terry a councilman application card and said, "You're going to a convention in Phoenix. Get your bags packed!" Obeying his older friend, Terry went to the LFTL convention, caught the vision and "jumped in with both feet." Over the next three decades he often attended banquets every night for a month during tours. Terry echoed the sentiments of many of the stalwart LFTL supporters who joined the program. Terry said, "It was Sam's vision that made the difference." Courtesy Robert Burke.*

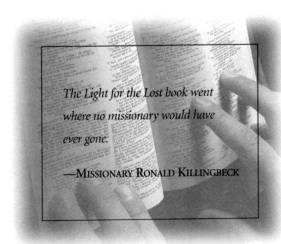

nine

It is Now a River

LIGHT FOR THE LOST WAS 20 YEARS OLD in 1973. In addressing the National LFTL Council in Phoenix, Arizona, J. Philip Hogan said:

> Twenty years ago, the Lord opened up a flowing well of life and blessing among laymen in the Assemblies of God. This flow has now become a river. Its course has carried it to every continent and to more than 90 countries of the world. This life-giving force has changed cultures, overcome the strongholds of pagan religions, and it flows on. Who knows to what distant shore this tide will reach? Those of us who have been privileged to witness its rise can only stand in gratitude and amazement and exclaim, "What hath God wrought!"

Annual LFTL fall tours raised substantial new commitments from Assemblies of God laymen across the country. An example of the success of the tours was the September 1973 blitz of Arkansas and Mississippi. In one weekend in Arkansas, funds were raised at a dozen night banquets and three breakfast rallies. Among the speakers for the events were Mississippi District Men's Department Director Clyde Griffith; Missionary Sam Balius; Mississippi LFTL Chairman Hubert Lowe; National LFTL Secretary Ellis Damiani; Arkansas District Superintendent Faye Hutchinson; District Secretary-Treasurer Raymond Thompson; Missionary Henry Culbreth; LFTL South Central Regional Vice President Chuck Freeman; and Gulf Coast Regional Vice President Hollis Lawson. Banquets or rallies were held in 14 of the 15 sections in Arkansas.

The following weekend in Mississippi many of the same speakers spread the message of the dire need for literature for overseas missions efforts. In all, LFTL tours were held in 32 districts of the Assemblies of God. The Northwest District produced a film, "Porto Alegre Story," a documentary on the success of LFTL in Brazil, to show to audiences to raise money for LFTL.

Sam continued to spend almost every weekend traveling across the country to participate in LFTL events. In 1973, his report indicated that he attended 46 banquets and rallies. He wrote, "In Los Gatos, California, God helped us raise over $10,000 in one day for LFTL. In Wisconsin, our goal was $10,000 but He gave us $15,000. In Indiana, the goal was $7,500 but again God gave us over $15,000. Praise be to God!"

LFTL headquarters in Springfield was inundated with good news reports as contributions rose each year, enabling the organization to provide more money for literature. Missionary Everett Ward in Paraguay wrote, "The presses are rolling. The setting is perfect now to launch our campaign. Praise the Lord for LFTL!" John Verbarendse, missionary to Ecuador, reported, "Through the printed word spiritual blindness is being overcome."

Here are examples of other notes of thanks received at the LFTL office just in September, 1973:

Every dime of the $3,000 we received went for literature. In four months the church averaged between 600-700 in attendance. I can truthfully say, had it not been for LFTL, we would not have this report to give.

—MISSIONARY-EVANGELIST R.E. JEFFERY IN QUITO, ECUADOR

In Korea, we used over 35,000 copies of our booklet for new converts, "Wonderful Things," for which funds were provided by LFTL. Thousands of souls responded to the invitation to receive Christ. More than 2,500 received the baptism in the Holy Spirit. In Sri Lanka, crowds swelled to 40,000 within one week. The final night the crowd was so vast we could not see the end of the throng. By the second night, they had used up 10,000 decision cards and we printed another 10,000. LFTL provided funds for the evangelistic literature for the great crusade which has added so many souls to the Kingdom.

—MISSIONARY WILLIAM CALDWELL IN KOREA

Among the hundreds who attended the Good News Crusade in Salitiga, Central Java, was four-year-old Adi Widodo and his mother. They had spent all they had on doctors with no apparent relief. One day I gave Adi's mother a LFTL tract and an invitation to the meeting. They came and God met them miraculously. As a result, the whole family found God. They were just a few of nearly 500 who responded to God's call.

—MISSIONARY HAROLD CARLBLOM IN SALATIGA, INDONESIA

The response to ICI courses is unbelievable. People are truly putting their faith in Christ as Savior. We want all those who work with LFTL to know that the struggling new nation of Bangladesh, with 75 million people, is feeling a new impact. A new light is shining in a very dark place. How grateful we are to LFTL for strengthening our hands for this task.

—Missionary Ronald S. Peck in Bangladesh

Just last week an old man from the middle bush country came to our house wanting to accept the Lord as his Savior. He is from a village more than a day's walk from the road. It has neither a school nor church. Apparently, a man who received one of the LFTL books read to the bushman from the book and because of this he has accepted Christ. The LFTL book went where no missionary would have ever gone.

—Missionary Ronald Killingbeck in New Hebrides

A printed lesson on the Holy Spirit fell into the hands of a Coptic priest who serves a church of 600, down-country from Cairo. While studying the lesson, he received the Holy Spirit. He became so excited he had all his church read the lesson. As a result, some 300 received the baptism in the Holy Spirit. Imagine what a stir this is causing in Egypt.

—Kenneth Alba, ICI Director for Egypt

Turkey is an example where there is an outpouring of the Holy Spirit unprecedented in the history of the country. In Iraq, which is closed to missionaries, a solid church

Ellis Damiani, left, and Sam look over trophies to be presented to outstanding councilmen and top-giving churches at the 1973 Light for the Lost national convention. Damiani served as national secretary of LFTL from 1970 to 1976.

is forming, all because of LFTL literature. Thank God for the printed literature which crosses the barriers of holy mountains, holy rivers, and holy walls.

—CHARLES GREENAWAY, FIELD SECRETARY FOR EUROPE

LFTL has invested $37,000 for the largest evangelization effort ever in West Africa. In several countries, Assemblies of God adherents will place millions of tracts and booklets in the hands of at least one million families.

—GERALD FALLEY, ASSEMBLIES OF GOD LITERATURE CENTER,
ACCRA, GHANA

In 1973, LFTL officials chose two major world cities, Buenos Aires, Argentina, and Hong Kong, as target cities to receive offerings from the National LFTL Day on May 6. A goal of $20,000 was set for the special day. The following year, Nairobi, Kenya, was chosen for emphasis.

Otto Wegner, a local banker, was introduced to LFTL in 1973 while attending Bethel Assembly of God in Milwaukee, Wisconsin. His mentor in the program was Wisconsin-Northern Michigan District LFTL Chairman Lud Oquist. Wegner said, "Brother Oquist kept the pressure on until I became a councilman." The moment Wegner enrolled, Sam's vision became his vision. He could see the results of his giving and the time spent assisting Oquist build the LFTL program in the district. When Oquist retired, Wegner took the reins of the highly successful district program that perennially finishes in the top ten districts in the nation in giving despite the fact that there are only 170 churches in the Wisconsin-Northern Michigan District.

Wegner served as a deacon for 25 years at Bethel Assembly, the same church that had sent missionary Julius Riske to Wegner's parents' hometown in eastern Germany, now Poland, in the 1930s. Wegner's parents were converted under the ministry of Riske and eventually emigrated to America, to Wisconsin. In 1995, Wegner completed the full circle by taking a LFTL Prayer Task Force team of eight people from Bethel Assembly back to Lodz, Poland, to minister in Polish churches and pray for the Assemblies of God missions work there.

ABOVE: *Lloyd Waterfield addresses a Light for the Lost banquet in southern California in 1973. Left to right, Warren Berwick, Waterfield, Bob Bruder, and Missionary Mark Buntain, the speaker for the banquet.*

RIGHT: *Sam presents the Light for the Lost Man-of-the-Year trophy to John Slye of Arlington, Virginia, at the 1974 national convention.*

Don Jacques attended his first LFTL national convention in 1974. He had learned of the program from his father-in-law, Hollis Lawson, one of the original supporters of Sam's vision. Lawson worked with Sam in LFTL in southern California since

In 1975, the Southern California District was high in national giving with Light for the Lost offerings of $208,027. Left to right, Lloyd Waterfield, Ray Neill, Bob Bruder, District Superintendent and later Assistant General Superintendent of the Assemblies of God Everett Stenhouse, Dwight Thompson, T.C. Cunningham, and Sam. Courtesy Everett Stenhouse.

the 1950s before he moved to Missouri in 1968. Lawson brought Sam's vision with him.

As a young layman attending the Assembly of God in Monett, Missouri, Jacques often carried the projector into churches across Missouri and surrounding states where Lawson presented the LFTL message with anointed preaching and films. The first time Jacques heard Sam speak, he was hooked. He remembered, "The reality of his vision became real to me. Sam was bigger than life, a hero of the faith, a man who had sold out to his vision."

Jacques moved to Springfield and stepped up his participation in LFTL tours in the Southern Missouri District. As his real estate business grew, he had more time to travel with Sam and other

LFTL spokesmen in other states and on Prayer Task Force and missionary trips to other lands.

Jacques is a strong believer in the theory that the success of LFTL can be traced to the "transferability" of Sam's vision in 1952. In times when Jacques grew weary from the long miles of travel promoting LFTL and the images of a lost and dying world grew dim, he prayed to God, "Let me again smell the burning flesh and hair of the men and women in Sam's vision. Let the smell permeate my senses and bring back my hunger to send the Word to millions of lost people in the world." Time and time again, Jacques says, "God has allowed me to renew the vision and strengthened me to go on."

Testimonies of the effectiveness of LFTL literature were recited by National LFTL Secretary Ellis Damiani in a special article

Light for the Lost councilmen honored at the 1975 national convention in Washington, D.C. Left to right, Sam; Phil Brachler, who served as national vice president from 1974 to 1976; Bob Bruder, who held every office available in LFTL from the 1970s to the 1990s; Phil Sondeno, national president and chairman from 1966 to 1973; and LFTL National Secretary Ellis Damiani.

in *The Pentecostal Evangel* June 15, 1975. Missionary John Weidman reported that two missionaries stopped in a West African town where they were approached by an elderly man who said, "I want to ask pardon for my sins." "What made you come here?" the missionaries asked. The man showed them a Good News tract, "Jesus Saves Sinners." He said, "I have come to accept Jesus!"

Damiani wrote that in one area of West Africa, 20,000 souls were won to the Lord after 2.5 million pieces of literature were used in Good News Crusades. Missionary Bob Hoskins in Beirut, Lebanon, reported that he had 300,000 students enrolled in ICI courses. He said it would be impossible to reach them through any other channel. From Nigeria, Missionary V.H. Shumway wrote that a half million tracts, printed in the Hausa language of northern Nigeria, were creating a spiritual revival with many souls saved.

Damiani concluded his special report with news from Missionary Bernhard Johnson in Brazil who conducted six major crusades with more than 41,500 persons accepting Christ as their Savior. Johnson said, "Because of LFTL, we were able to distribute

3,122,000 pieces of gospel literature. What did we ever do in years past before LFTL came into existence?"

LFTL raised $498,632 nationally in 1973. The list of LFTL councilmen mushroomed to 1,300.

In 1975, Tim and Cheryl Dewey wrote a song called "Light for the Lost." The chorus of the song succinctly told the LFTL story:

Help send the light for the lost,
Tell them Jesus really loves them,
Each day millions are dying without him;
Help send the light for the lost,
Tell them Jesus really loves them,
And that one day we all will be with Him.

The Southern California District swept councilman honors at the national Light for the Lost convention in 1976. Left to right, Ray Neill; Roy Sapp, pastor of First Assembly in Wilmington, California; Jerry Terry; Bob Bruder; and Tim Tyler.

In November 1975, Damiani resigned his post as national LFTL secretary to become pastor of an Assemblies of God church in Poughkeepsie, New York. Harold W. Walls, a veteran Arkansas pastor who had spearheaded the growth of LFTL in the Arkansas District, succeeded him.

Ray Rachels came to the Southern California District in the mid 1970s and Sam was one of the first persons he met. Rachels, who has served many years as district superintendent, was captivated by the mission of LFTL. He remembered, "It was, and is, a great ministry that allows a layman to 'get his hand around it' and 'feel' the program."

"Brutally confrontational" was the way Rachels described Sam's methods. "He was a true genius for putting his finger on the right program at the right time. He was a dominant speaker, wasted no time, and cut to the chase about the need for literature overseas."

Rachels bought into Sam's idea that LFTL banquets provided the most effective means to enlist new councilman and solicit faith promises. Rachels observed, "The banquets were successful because common laymen saw other good men, common laymen like themselves, who were motivated by Sam's vision. It made it easy for men to identify with their brothers and get on the LFTL bandwagon."

"Sam was successful because his goals were always above everyone around him," Rachels said.

Sam's insurance business continued to flourish. He and his eldest son James formed an insurance partnership in 1976. The business was called Cochran and Son. Sam spent more time as an insurance consultant and created a separate company, Sam Cochran and Company. He advised individuals and companies on mutual funds, insurance, and retirement programs. He founded the American Society of Certified Insurance Consultants. He served on the Board of Trustees of Southern California College, and the governing boards of the Griffith Foundation at Ohio State

A young soldier reads Light for the Lost literature received from Italian Christians witnessing on the streets of Padova, Italy, in 1976.

University and the Captains of Industry in Los Angeles, and was Western Regional Secretary of the Gamma Iota Sigma Fraternity. He also was a member of the Foreign Missions Board of the General Council of the Assemblies of God.

ABOVE: *During the Tennessee District fall tour in the 1970s, record Light for the Lost pledges were received. Left to right, David Wharton, Tennessee Men's Ministries director; Harold Walls, national LFTL secretary; Ralph M. Crass, sectional Men's Ministries director; and Paul Sharpe, Tennessee LFTL chairman.*

One of the most densely populated cities in the world, Jakarta, Indonesia, was chosen as the 1976 LFTL target city. Missionary Jim Anderson directed hundreds of teams of young people, with shoulder bags filled with tracts, to canvas busy intersections throughout the city. As signal lights stopped traffic, the youth moved swiftly to each vehicle to hand out tracts to drivers and passengers. One evening when traffic was very heavy, the youth could not handle the load. Two non-Christian policemen helped them by taking handfuls of tracts and passing them to motorists. When everyone had received a tract, the policemen blew their whistles and directed traffic on.

After one campaign in a Jakarta neighborhood, a man came looking for the address of the Assemblies of God church which was stamped on the tract. Samuel Pribodi, a medical doctor and deacon of the church, saw the young man searching for the

give me the book!

address and asked if he could help. The man showed him the tract and replied, "A young man gave this to me yesterday at the market. I do not fully understand it but each time I read it I want to cry." Dr. Pribodi explained the way of salvation and the man readily accepted Christ.

Pastors of the three top-giving LFTL churches in 1976 agreed that LFTL was good for their churches. In *Advance Magazine*, Pastor Roy Sapp of First Assembly in Wilmington, California, said, "Sam's vision was a sovereign move of God to begin the program. It is necessary in light of present world conditions."

BELOW: *Sam leads the 1978 national Light for the Lost convention in prayer.*

The guest of honor at the 1978 national Light for the Lost convention was Assemblies of God General Superintendent Thomas F. Zimmerman. (Left to right) Hollis Lawson, Zimmerman, and Sam.

g i v e   m e   t h e   b o o k !

Pastor Charles Crabtree of Bethel Church in San Jose, California, said, "I became interested in LFTL because of my personal desire to go into missions. Instead of giving me a 'green light' to go as a missionary, the Lord impressed upon me the need to build strong missionary churches. I see a great need for the written Word."

Finally, Pastor Glen Cole of Evergreen Christian Center in Olympia, Washington, said, "LFTL provides great tools for our ministry. Without the help of LFTL, there would be much less of an impact in the Assemblies of God world missions program."

LFTL funds were critical to the worldwide success of ICI and its correspondence ministry. Missionary Angelo Nesta reported from Italy in 1976, "Because of the American laymen giving, ICI in Italy became operational, people were saved, others were helped spiritually, and churches were blessed. Italy started with little funds; but when money was needed to print evangelism literature, thousands of dollars were made available from LFTL."

In February 1977, Sam underwent open-heart surgery. After a few days in the hospital he told one caller, "I feel like I'm 20 again." Prayer warriors throughout the world remembered Sam daily during his recovery.

In 1977, La Paz, Bolivia, was the LFTL target city. The National Council of LFTL convened for its annual convention in Seattle, Washington. Assemblies of God General Superintendent Thomas F. Zimmerman delivered the keynote address. Robert Bruder was reelected national LFTL chairman. John Slye of Arlington, Virginia, was selected as national president; Tim Tyler of Los Alamitos, California, was reelected as national vice-chairman; and Sam continued in his role as executive vice president, a position created exclusively for him for as long as he wanted.

LFTL celebrated its silver anniversary in 1978. Speakers at the national convention in San Jose, California, included Sam;

Oklahoma District Superintendent Robert Goggin; David Crabtree, pastor of First Assembly in Des Moines, Iowa; and Bernhard Johnson, missionary-evangelist from Brazil.

Donald Strong of Pasco, Washington, was named Pastor-of-the-Year. LFTL District Superintendent-of-the-Year was William H. Robertson of the Southern California District, which also was named the District-of-the-Year. Evergreen Christian Center in Olympia, Washington, was the top-giving LFTL church in the nation. Lou Cousineau of Pasco, Washington, was the LFTL Councilman-of-the-Year. It was announced that for the first time the number of LFTL councilmen had topped 2,000.

Reports from the 1978 fall LFTL tour were encouraging. The LFTL newsletter, *Unitgram*, contained stories of several districts exceeding goals in banquets. Speakers in the tours included John Slye, Harold Walls, and Phil Brauchler in Georgia; David Crabtree and Ellis Damiani in Indiana; Lawrence Turner in Nebraska; Robert Mackish and Morris Plotts in Ohio; Fred Hallberg in South Dakota; and Harold Walls in Wyoming.

In early 1979, LFTL National Secretary Harold Walls resigned to become pastor of First Assembly of God in Little Rock, Arkansas. He was succeeded by Dwain W. Jones, a former missionary to Tonga and veteran pastor in several districts.

India's fourth largest city, Madras, was targeted to receive LFTL funds in 1979. Teams of workers saturated the city with millions of pieces of LFTL literature. The workers gave a personal witness and left a packet of information that included a portion of the Word of God and an invitation to a local Assemblies of God church. A coordinated follow-up ministry also required much literature. David Stewart, the only missionary in the city of nearly four million people, credited the LFTL blitz with the establishment of five new churches in the city. A decade later, the church in Madras, which had grown to a membership of several thousand, was recognized worldwide for its incredible emphasis on prayer.

At the 1979 LFTL convention, Foreign Missions Executive Director J. Philip Hogan delivered a stirring assessment of the success of the literature distribution program started so humbly by Sam 26 years before. Hogan pointed to Burma, closed to missionaries for two decades, where LFTL literature had resulted in so many new souls coming to the Lord that 26 churches had been founded. Hogan reported that in two totally Muslim provinces in Malaysia where Christians were not even allowed to get off an airplane at the airport, a unique method of evangelization had occurred. LFTL material was sent to people in the provinces in unmarked envelopes. Six thousand people responded with requests to enroll in ICI courses.

Hogan said LFTL played a major role in phenomenal growth of the Assemblies of God in Africa. In Upper Volta, the number of adherents tripled in five years. Next door in Nigeria, the Assemblies of God grew from 60,000 to 154,000 in five years. But Hogan saved most of his plaudits for the LFTL effort in Latin America:

> We gave out 1.2 million pieces of literature in Guatemala, we had 205 revival meetings going on at the same time, thousands were saved. We had 11,000 converts in 62 crusades last month in the Dominican Republic. This week, saints of that country are following up every convert card to give them LFTL literature.
>
> In the interior of Central America, missionary pilots flew a very loud airplane over villages, scaring occupants of houses into the streets where they were met by national workers with sacks of LFTL literature. The missionary in the airplane, via a powerful loud speaker, directs people to go into their houses and retrieve a small hand mirror and beam a signal to the plane if they want prayer. It's unbelievable. The stories of outright miracles that have taken place from that sky pilot praying for the people. We pray

for the mayor, we pray for the chief of police, we pray for the government, we even pray for the Catholic priests.

In closing, Hogan challenged LFTL councilmen to begin to plan to reach the masses of people in China. He predicted that the country would be open to evangelization. Hogan said, "Down in the human heart, crushed by the tempter, feelings lie buried that grace can restore. I have a feeling that if we get enough of the Book in there, these young people will forget their shipyards and their airplanes and their quest for a higher standard of living. In that spiritual vacuum, I believe that God will light the greatest whirlwind, prairie fire revival that ever swept a nation."

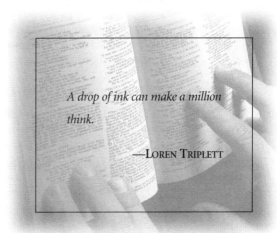

A drop of ink can make a million think.

—Loren Triplett

ten

Chain Reactions

GOD HAS USED HOLY "CHAIN REACTIONS" to allow Sam's vision to be replicated throughout the nation and the world. An example is how Joe Livesay of Lafayette, Indiana, became involved in LFTL in 1978. Livesay was sent to a LFTL breakfast by his pastor, Charles Hackett. The speaker was Ball State University Professor Arnold Cirtin who had been signed up as a LFTL councilman years before by Ray Neill, one of Sam's early "disciples."

As Cirtin showed the original LFTL promotional film, the Holy Spirit dealt with Livesay's heart. When the house lights came back up, Livesay filled out a councilman application card.

Shortly, Livesay was asked to host a LFTL banquet in his home church, First Assembly of Lafayette, where he was men's director. In the church's first major effort to support LFTL, $15,000 was pledged. A year later, Cirtin tabbed Livesay as district LFTL director. In his first year, district-wide giving to LFTL was only $34,000.

In 2000, Livesay was still district director and Indiana churches gave $332,000 to LFTL. His perennial speech at LFTL banquets and rallies was centered around the question, "Can one person make a difference on the mission field?"

There is also another kind of "chain reaction" involved in LFTL. It is the God-breathed multiplication of the printing of a single piece of gospel literature.

ABOVE: *Many times, Joe Livesay invited Sam to Indiana to speak at rallies and banquets. Sam often promoted Light for the Lost at the Indiana District Council. Livesay reflected, "Sam's anointed approach worked because it harnessed laymen and gave them a genuine opportunity to do something for Jesus Christ. Sam always looked our men in the eye and boldly asked, 'Do you want to help fulfill the Great Commission?'"* **Courtesy Robert Burke.**

Two decades ago, Nelda Ammons, the Division of Foreign Missions LFTL coordinator, shared with readers of *The Pentecostal Evangel* stories she had collected of the successes of LFTL around the world. There was a tailor who lived high on the side of a mountain in Costa Rica. One day as Marcos sat working at his ancient Singer sewing machine, he heard a paper fluttering in the crack between two boards of his home. It was siesta time so he stopped the machine, pulled the paper from the wall, and began to read.

A 1978 Light for the Lost promotion brochure.

The message on the paper gripped Marcos's heart. Never before had he heard such a powerful story. An address stamped on the paper led him to a church where he found a pastor preaching the same message. Marcos accepted Christ and a short time later answered the call of God into the ministry. He donated his house to the church. With the proceeds from the sale of his sewing machine, Marcos set out for a neighboring village to pioneer a church.

Within two years Marcos built eight new churches. And the "chain reaction" had not stopped. As he continued to pioneer churches, he was elected general superintendent of the Assemblies of God in Costa Rica, a position he held for two decades. In the early 1980s, more than 50 Costa Rican Assemblies of God ministers were personal converts of the former tailor who learned of Christ through one single piece of LFTL literature.

By 1980, the average cost of a LFTL tract was only two cents. Nelda Ammons asked, "How many people find Christ as a result of one tract?" She answered her own question, "No one really knows."

As annual LFTL contributions increased dramatically, so did the results of massive literature distribution campaigns.

LFTL provided literature for a major Good News Crusade planned for Bangkok, Thailand, in the summer of 1980. In *The Pentecostal Evangel* the Sunday before the annual Light for the Lost Day on May 4, National Secretary Dwain Jones pleaded with the nation's Assemblies of

Dwain Jones, national Light for the Lost secretary from 1979 to 1983, looks on as Wesley Hurst, Far East field secretary for the Assemblies of God, shows one of the 10,000 New Testaments printed in Chinese with LFTL funds in 1979.

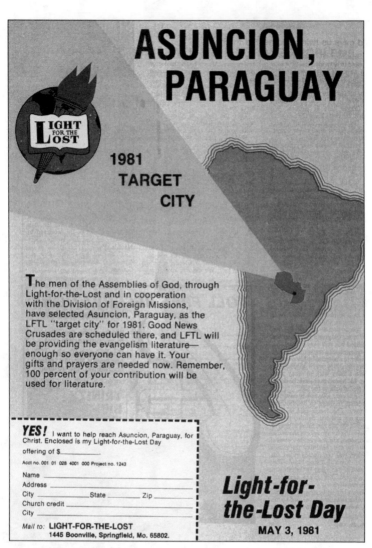

ASUNCION, PARAGUAY

1981 TARGET CITY

The men of the Assemblies of God, through Light-for-the-Lost and in cooperation with the Division of Foreign Missions, have selected Asuncion, Paraguay, as the LFTL "target city" for 1981. Good News Crusades are scheduled there, and LFTL will be providing the evangelism literature—enough so everyone can have it. Your gifts and prayers are needed now. Remember, 100 percent of your contribution will be used for literature.

YES! I want to help reach Asuncion, Paraguay, for Christ. Enclosed is my Light-for-the-Lost Day offering of $_____.

Acct no. 001 01 028 4001 000 Project no. 1243

Name _____
Address _____
City _____ State _____ Zip _____
Church credit _____
City _____

Mail to: **LIGHT-FOR-THE-LOST**
1445 Boonville, Springfield, Mo. 65802.

Light-for-the-Lost Day

MAY 3, 1981

The 1981 LFTL target city was Asuncion, Paraguay. Assemblies of God Latin American Field Director Loren Triplett said, "Literature is extremely important in this project. There is no way to fully describe its effectiveness, and people are eager to receive it. None will be wasted." LFTL was on the front line of the targeting of Asuncion. Hundreds of thousands of special pieces of Paraguayan evangelistic literature were distributed in Paraguay, one of the poorest countries of the world. This full-page contribution request appeared in The Pentecostal Evangel. *Courtesy* The Pentecostal Evangel.

God churches to support the Thailand effort. He wrote, "Our missionaries are ready. They are looking to us to fill their hands with the literature that brings the good news of Jesus Christ and His salvation. Bangkok has over four million inhabitants. In scores of other cities and towns, the gospel has never been preached."

At the 1980 annual convention in Tulsa, Oklahoma, Tim Tyler, an executive at Douglas Aircraft Company and former lieutenant colonel in the United States Air Force, was elected national chairman. Other officers were Chuck Freeman, Oklahoma City, national president, and David Burdine, Colorado Springs, Colorado, National vice chairman. Sam was reelected by acclamation as executive vice president. The

Assemblies of God General Superintendent Thomas F. Zimmerman, right, was an enthusiastic supporter of Light for the Lost. He and Sam developed a strong personal relationship. Sam said, "As with other general superintendents, Brother Zimmerman had an 'open door' policy for me. If LFTL needed something, I walked into his office and asked for it."

national LFTL board was expanded to 50 members so that each Assembles of God district had a representative.

The Southern California District again won District-of-the-Year honors by giving $217,642 to LFTL. The first-place church in giving was also a repeat, Evergreen Christian Center in Olympia, Washington, with LFTL offerings of $25,925. J.W. Ellsworth, pastor of Eastland Assembly in Tulsa, Oklahoma, was named Pastor-of-the-Year, with 41 new councilmen signed up in his church. The Councilman-of-the-Year Award went to Jerry Lee of San Jose, California, who enlisted 53 new councilmen the previous year.

LFTL councilmen met in national convention in San Diego, California, in April 1981. The four top officers of LFTL were reelected. Speakers included Northern California-Nevada District Superintendent William Vickery, Southern California District Superintendent Everett Stenhouse, LFTL Potomac District Representative John Slye, and Missionary-Evangelist Wayne Francis.

Stenhouse was named Superintendent-of-the-Year. Charles Crabtree of Bethel Church in San Jose, California, received the Pastor-of-the-Year Award; Loren Ennis of Casper, Wyoming, was named Councilman-of-the-Year; and Men's Ministries Director-of-the-Year was Bruce Strong of Casper, Wyoming.

The Executive LFTL Committee approved the spending of $20,000 to develop the ICI course, "Great Questions of Life," for Muslims. Production of a new LFTL film was also approved.

LFTL chose Yaounde, Cameroon, as the target city for 1982. In a special appeal for funds for the African city, Loren Triplett wrote in *The Evangel*, "A new literate believes what he reads. The first time a man picks up a piece of paper and it talks to him because he has just learned to read, he believes what the paper says. No one can talk him out of accepting it as fact. Therefore, the most

David Burdine was national Light for the Lost chairman from 1982 to 1984. He later founded Bethesda Ministries.

important issue in our world today is: Who is going to get to these new literates first, and with what?"

Triplett recognized the worth of the contribution LFTL was making. He wrote, "Wherever beachheads have been set up by missionaries, wherever successful penetration has been made into heathendom, it was been done by the help of the printed page and the written Word of God."

Triplett told the story of a businessman in Brazil who walked by a church where he was handed a tract by a young boy. The man tore the tract to shreds. When he got home, he found a scrap of the tract clinging to his clothes. On it were printed three words: "And God said."

Don Wilson served in four different Light for the Lost positions in the 1980s and 1990s. He was training coordinator, councilman coordinator, and either national president or national chairman from 1986 to 1992.

Curiosity gripped him. Who were these people, he wondered, *and how could they know what God said?* Twenty-four hours later, the man went by the same church and asked for a copy of the tract. In a short time, he was saved and became a lay preacher.

David Burdine of Colorado Springs, Colorado, was elected national chairman at the 1982 LFTL convention in Denver, Colorado. Chuck Freeman was elected national vice chairman and Don Jacques of Springfield, Missouri, was elected national president.

Don Wilson of San Jose, California, an insurance broker, was named national training coordinator, a new position, and was

A 1983 brochure encouraged councilmen to establish "steak teams" to cater annual Light for the Lost banquets.

tabbed to serve on the executive committee. Regional vice presidents elected were: Gulf—David Wharton, Old Hickory, Tennessee; Great Lakes—David Barth, Salem, Oregon; North Central—Carrol Wilson, Faribault, Minnesota; Northeast—Ralph Borden, Falls Church, Virginia; Northwest—Ray Radford, Bothel, Washington; South Central—James Holt, Tulsa, Oklahoma; Southeast—Rick Coburn, Kernersville, North Carolina; and Southwest—Ray Neill, Long Beach, California.

Charles Hackett of First Assembly of God, Lafayette, Indiana, was named LFTL Pastor-of-the-Year in 1982. The top-giving church, with $46,937, was Bethel Church in San Jose, California, where Charles Crabtree was pastor. Southern California was number one in district-wide giving, with offerings of $345,346. Joe Livesay was the Councilman-of-the-Year. He enrolled 148 councilmen the previous year.

LFTL councilmen contributed $11,000 to a special project in 1982 to produce a special book for military outreaches. It was *The Dave Roever Story*, an attractive pictorial booklet designed to have a strong appeal and convey a simple salvation message. More than 50,000 copies were distributed free of charge to military personnel. Roever was an Assemblies of God evangelist who had a powerful testimony of miraculous healing from near fatal injuries suffered while in Vietnam.

Reginald Stone, right, shares Light for the Lost literature with a national pastor in Africa. Stone was national LFTL secretary from 1984 to 1987.

Sam was awarded a PhD in business in 1984 from the California Graduate School.

One of Europe's tourist meccas, Amsterdam, the Netherlands, was targeted for a LFTL literature blitz in 1983, the 30th anniversary of the founding of the missions literature program.

Sam, LFTL National Secretary Dwain Jones, Missionary to Brazil Bernhard Johnson, and Pastor Charles Hackett were keynote speakers at the 1983 convention in Springfield. Councilmen were elated when Sam announced that, for the first time, the number of LFTL councilmen exceeded 5,000. In the previous 12 months, LFTL had raised $1,734,000, one hundred percent of which went to print literature for Assemblies of God missionaries.

In March 1984, Reginald A. Stone succeeded Dwain Jones as national LFTL secretary. Stone had both pastored and served as a missionary to Uruguay. Jones became national Men's Ministries secretary. Ernest W. "Ernie" Lawrence was appointed Men's Ministries Department editor and was given responsibility for editing two LFTL publications, including *Spotlight,* and promoting LFTL.

For the third time in the history of LFTL, Mexico City, which had become the world's most populous city, was named as the target city for special fund-raising efforts in May 1984. Ernie Lawrence wrote, "The mission is to make an impact on 18 million people. The first strike task force is already in action, and ammunition is being issued. That ammunition is not explosive shells nor nuclear warheads—it is much more powerful. It is the printed Word of God."

For the first time the Division of Foreign Missions targeted a city for more than just one year. Mexico City was the focal point for three years. LFTL men's prayer teams went to Mexico City and simply prayed for the city. The action teams, paying their own expenses, spent a week praying and working with local pastors and laymen in home and street evangelism, tent crusades, and church planting projects.

Media restrictions in Mexico made it nearly impossible to use radio or television to publicize services. Tons of LFTL literature, including gospel tracts and flyers announcing revivals, were used to prepare for the target city project. Over three million pieces of literature, at a cost of $300,000, brought eternal life and hope to thousands of Mexico City residents.

Manila, the Philippines, was revisited as a LFTL target city in 1985. A LFTL Prayer Task Force, led by Chuck Freeman, visited some of the ten sites chosen for tent crusades and eventual church building projects.

In 1986, LFTL focused on evangelism efforts in Harare, Zimbabwe, formerly Rhodesia. LFTL funds paid for the saturation of the African city of nearly 700,000 people with gospel literature.

By 1986 LFTL was pushing back the darkness in 136 countries. From Ivory Coast in Africa came the story of the founding of a church because of a single LFTL tract. Somehow, through the grace of God, a tract on salvation found its way to a remote village. Several young people began meeting together and discussing the contents of the tract. One of the villagers made his way across country to a town with an Assemblies of God mission station. He accepted Christ and went back with the joyous story of salvation. At last count, more than 100 people in that village attended weekly church services.

Bill Strickland became LFTL national secretary in the summer of 1987. Reginald Stone left LFTL to become director of the Residence Advance School of Theology in Lima, Peru. Strickland served as a missionary to Honduras for ten years and knew Latin America well.

Bombay, India, the gateway to nearly a billion people in India, was targeted by LFTL in 1987. More than two-thirds of the world's eighth largest city lived in one-room tenements, literally living out their existence without hope. Believing that "it was the hour" for Bombay, the Assemblies of God asked Evangelist Bernhard Johnson to hold a series of crusades. Johnson said, "We do not believe in cursing the darkness of heathenism, but in striking a light in the midst of the darkness."

At one crusade meeting, Johnson asked how many of the thousands gathered were present because someone knocked on their door and gave them a piece of literature and invited them to the meeting. Johnson was shocked when more than 80 percent of the throng raised their hands, indicating it was the LFTL literature that brought them to the crusade.

For the second time in the 1980s, Bangkok, Thailand, a city of spiritual darkness, was chosen for a literature evangelism blitz in 1988. Ninety-six percent of the people in the city of 6.5 million were Buddhists, difficult to convert. Robert W. Houlihan, Far East field director for the Assemblies of God Division of Foreign Missions, expressed how important LFTL was in breaking through the veil of Buddhism. Houlihan said, "It is important people receive an evangelism tract during revival meetings. These tracts are often the beginning of a breakthrough in this stronghold of Buddhism."

Assemblies of God General Superintendent G. Raymond Carlson addressed LFTL councilmen at the 35th national convention in 1988. Don Wilson was elected national chairman; Otto Wegner was elected national vice chairman; Robert Bruder was elected national president; and Sam was reelected to his perennial post as executive vice president. Joe Livesay was chosen as councilman coordinator. Regional vice presidents elected were: Gulf—Alan Taylor; North Central—Lud Oquist; Northeast— Will Burrows; Northwest—Delmer Westerfield; South Central— James Holt; and Southwest—Bill Davis.

Councilman-of-the-Year honors went to three men who enrolled the most new LFTL councilmen the previous year.

Jerry Freeman of Oklahoma City was first in the nation, with 83, followed by Glen Gilbertson and Nick Easter.

Alton Garrison, pastor of First Assembly in North Little Rock, Arkansas, was honored as the Pastor-of-the-Year for showing the largest increase in the number of LFTL councilmen.

In 1989, Evan Paul was named administrative assistant for LFTL. He assumed responsibility for editing *Spotlight*, the monthly LFTL newsletter, and coordinating the Overseas Prayer Task Force ministries, a program involving two teams of men a year in prayer, fasting, and witnessing in other countries.

The focus of the annual National Light for the Lost Day in May 1989 was Kingston, Jamaica. Before preaching crusades were held, a LFTL Prayer Task Force was dispatched to the island nation to pray for the 13 Assemblies of God missionaries and 89 credentialed national ministers who pastored the 65 churches and 34 outstations scattered around the island.

> *We do not believe in cursing the darkness of heathenism, but in striking a light in the midst of the darkness.*
>
> —BERNHARD JOHNSON

eleven

a Decade of Harvest

SAM RETIRED FROM AN ACTIVE LFTL LEADERSHIP position in 1989, but he did not retire from his ministry. His heart still burned with the message of taking the printed Word to the whole world. Even though he was at an age when most men retired and slowed down, Sam continued to devote his time and energy to building the LFTL councilmen rolls and adding to the growing contributions to the literature fund. He continued to speak at countless banquets, rallies, and church services. Sam and Geri faithfully attended Christian Assembly in Aliso Viejo, California, where Darrell Ward was pastor.

The Assemblies of God designated the 1990s as "The Decade of Harvest." Eight decades of progress had not dimmed the fellowship's leaders' strong defense of the Pentecostal message. Following the stirring admonition of Daddy Welch at the beginning of the movement, Assemblies of God officials renewed their

Sam retired from an active leadership role in Light for the Lost in 1989. He was honored at a reception at the 1989 national LFTL convention.

dedication to reach the whole world with the gospel of Jesus Christ. Arm in arm with missionaries and evangelists, LFTL literature was sent by the ton to most every country of the world.

"Pulling down Satan's strongholds" was the way LFTL Secretary Strickland described the 1990 effort to target the African city of Lilongwe, Malawi. A Prayer Task Force preceded revival crusades.

While literature blitzes were financed with LFTL funds in Malawi, a LFTL Prayer Task Force, 17 councilmen strong, spent a week in Freetown, Sierra Leone, fasting and praying with missionaries and national leaders. Their prayers were for Evangelist Ben Tipton's Good News Crusade. The first night more than 600 people gave their lives to Christ. As Strickland wrote, "Satan's stronghold was beginning to fall."

LFTL Prayer Task Forces were sent to all points of the globe in 1990. Teams went to Dhaka, Bangladesh; Calcutta, India; San Salvador, El Salvador; Quito, Ecuador; Lima, Peru; Buenos Aires, Argentina; Sao Paulo, Brazil; Kingston, Jamaica; and Monterrey, Mexico.

Bill McGuire, a salesman from Kansas City, Kansas, described a Prayer Task Force, "I never return home the same. God has given me a burden for the people. I would encourage every Christian man to get involved in LFTL. Going on a Prayer Task Force trip will change them."

LEFT: *At the 1989 convention, Sam received a special letter from General Superintendent G. Raymond Carlson, left, commemorating Sam's 250th Light for the Lost councilman enrollee.*

RIGHT: *Wayne Long of Oklahoma City, Oklahoma, right, receives the Councilman-of-the-Year Award in 1989 from Assemblies of God General Superintendent G. Raymond Carlson.*

LEFT: *Missionary-Evangelist David Grant was a frequent speaker at Light for the Lost rallies and banquets and national LFTL conventions.*

CENTER: *From its inception, J. Philip Hogan, executive director of the Assemblies of God worldwide missions effort, was a vigorous supporter of Light for the Lost.*

RIGHT: *One of the speakers at the 1989 national Light for the Lost convention was Bob Houlihan, Asia Pacific field director for the Assemblies of God Division of Foreign Missions.*

Virgil Cook, a retired optometrist from Mena, Arkansas, compared his Prayer Task Force with the 25 other missions trips he had made over a quarter century. Cook said, "I went before as an optometrist; this time I went to pray. I never stopped weeping the morning we spent with the missionaries."

LFTL councilmen raised $3,312,564 for evangelism literature in 1991. The list of councilmen mushroomed to 5,177. They contributed $634,422 to administer the national program. Men's Ministries Secretary Ken Riemenschneider announced that 2,810 churches contributed to LFTL. Of the total giving, $198,210.83 was designated for home missions projects. The remainder went to purchase gospel literature for the 1,600 foreign missionaries of the Assemblies of God.

Suva, the capital of the Fiji Islands in the South Pacific, was targeted by LFTL in 1991. Missionary Randy Carlson described the hunger for gospel literature, "At a recent meeting of national pastors, I announced that we had tracts available on a back table.

A Bolivian man poses with Light for the Lost literature in 1990. "The Great Questions of Life," printed in Spanish, was duplicated millions of times for hungry souls in Latin America. The book was an integral part of the International Correspondence Institute (ICI) courses that have reported millions of conversions. George Flattery, a native of Three Sands, Oklahoma, was the major driving force behind the creation of ICI. Courtesy The Pentecostal Evangel.

LEFT: *Light for the Lost national conventions traditionally feature special programs for wives of councilmen. Special speakers and tours of the convention city are often featured. These ladies were part of an old-fashioned fashion show at the 1990 LFTL convention.*

RIGHT: *Ron Maddux was a speaker at the 1990 Light for the Lost convention in Charlotte, North Carolina.*

You would have thought there was gold on the table as people rushed back to get materials. Indeed, these tracts are as precious as gold, often being the most important tool the pastors possess to take the gospel back to share in their villages." A Prayer Task Force was also organized as part of the blitz on Fiji.

In 1991, 22 LFTL Prayer Task Force teams visited cities in almost every country of Latin America and in the Cape Verde Islands, West Africa, and Russia. In Honduras, a team met at the crusade tent each morning, paired with nationals, and walked the

Sam makes an appeal for Light for the Lost pledges during the 1991 tour in the Kansas District of the Assemblies of God where Jon Hollis was men's director.

streets placing literature in the hands of people who had never heard the gospel. Pastor Larry Meeks recalled, "We returned to the hotel to spend the afternoons in prayer. As we fasted and prayed, we were spiritually and physically renewed. It seemed that God orchestrated our times of prayer and prepared us for the evening rallies." Over 400 people attended the first night's rally.

In March 1992, a nine-member LFTL team from the Potomac District of the Assemblies of God

Jerry Parsley, Assemblies of God field director for Eurasia, was a speaker at the 1991 national Light for the Lost convention.

Light for the Lost councilmen enjoyed a golf outing the day before the official start of the 1992 national convention in Springfield, Missouri. Evangel Assembly of God in Fair Grove, Missouri, provided a church van for transportation for the golfers, an example of how local churches provide substantial support when a national LFTL convention comes to their area.

give me the book!

spent a week distributing the *Book of Life*, a chronological account of the life of Christ, in Granada, Nicaragua, one of the oldest cities in Central America. The team placed a copy in 99 percent of the homes visited. For the first time, Nicaraguan schools were open for distribution of the book. Word spread faster than the book distribution. People ran into the streets or waited at the door for their free copy.

Benny W. Ferguson took over daily supervision of LFTL as national LFTL coordinator in July 1992. Ferguson had pastored churches in North Texas, Oklahoma, and Missouri.

LFTL targeted Seville, Spain in 1992. A LFTL prayer team converged on Seville, the sight of the 1992 World's

Sam had brain surgery in 1992. After the successful surgery, he and Geri traveled to Ireland for a long-awaited vacation.

ABOVE: *African children read Light for the Lost literature, often their first introduction to the story of Christ. Courtesy* The Pentecostal Evangel.

Fair, celebrating the 500th anniversary of Columbus' discovery of the new world.

"Reach Them at Any Cost," was the theme of the 1992 LFTL national convention in Springfield. Speakers included Missionary to Ireland Gary Davidson, Bill Strickland, Mission of Mercy Representative Dwain Jones, Pastor Alton Garrison, and LFTL Vice President Robert Bruder.

In one of his first reports in *The Pentecostal Evangel* after being named national LFTL coordinator in 1992, Benny Ferguson wrote that LFTL was "marching off the map," reaching peoples that no one thought possible a decade before. One example was Mongolia, one of the most closed nations on earth. Several thousand New Testaments, printed by LFTL funds, were printed in Mongolia.

give me the book!

Ferguson said, "God is breaking down barriers in areas where many believed it would never happen. We must be prepared to move forward and march into uncharted territory."

Don Jacques, LFTL national president, led a Prayer Task Force team into Indonesia in 1992. Malaysian laymen joined Jacques's team and expressed an interest in setting up their own national LFTL program.

Quito, Ecuador, was chosen as the LFTL target city in 1993. People prayed that the LFTL literature saturation and evangelistic effort in a rented theater and adjacent building complex would be the beginning of a major move of God's spirit among the 11 million people of Ecuador.

BELOW: *"Precious" Light for the Lost literature is handed out to new converts in Africa. Courtesy* The Pentecostal Evangel.

LFTL giving jumped to $5.28 million in 1992, nearly a $2 million increase over the previous year. Contributions came from 56 districts of the Assemblies of God.

Oklahoma City, Oklahoma, was the site of the 40th LFTL national convention in April 1993. Division of Foreign Missions Executive Director Loren Triplett addressed a LFTL World Prayer Meeting banquet. Another featured speaker was Prince Guneratnam, general superintendent of the Assemblies of God in Malaysia.

Benny Ferguson and the LFTL National Council established a LFTL Junior Councilmen program in 1994. Boys who had completed the LFTL Advanced Award in Royal Rangers, the Assemblies of God boys program in local churches, could sign up as junior councilmen and participate in missions through LFTL. The junior councilmen program was responsible for the distribution of 250,000 Bible portions to young people in the inner cities of America.

Bill Wilson, pastor of Metro Assembly of God in Brooklyn, New York, testified to the effectiveness of inner-city literature distribution. Wilson said, "A child took a flyer home and left it on the table. That night his mother came into the living room, planning to take her life. At the point of her suicide, her eyes fell on a piece of colorful paper. She read the flyer. The Holy Sprit did His work and she accepted Christ."

In 1994, Charles Crabtree, assistant general superintendent of the Assemblies of God and director of the Decade of Harvest, talked about the importance of LFTL. Crabtree wrote, "As a pastor, I built my local men's ministries around the LFTL councilmen program. I discovered that a men's program could not be sustained without a fundamental purpose. LFTL provided that purpose."

Antananarivo, a city of 1.3 million and capital of Madagascar, was the LFTL target city in 1994.

The Excelsior Hotel in Little Rock, Arkansas, hosted the 1994 national LFTL convention. Speakers included Charles Crabtree;

Chuck Freeman; Benny Ferguson; Terry Raburn, national director of the Assemblies of God Division of Church Ministries; and Robert Mackish, missions area representative for Eastern Europe.

In 1994 LFTL elections, Don Jacques was returned to office as national president for another two year term, as was Vice President Joe Livesay. Chuck Freeman left the executive committee after two terms. He was succeeded by his son, Jerry Freeman, who had learned the LFTL message by standing long hours at his father's side, cooking ribs and steaks for LFTL banquets and rallies, and seeing the results of evangelistic campaigns around the world. Other vice presidents elected were Len Ventling and Otto Wegner.

Mike Purkey of Kansas City, Kansas, was recognized as the LFTL Pastor-of-the-Year. Fayette Miller was Councilman-of-the-Year. Ray Rachels of the Southern California District, was the District Superintendent-of-the-Year, and Phil Brauchler, the Peninsular Florida LFTL chairman, received a plaque for enrolling 250 councilmen. Capital Christian Center in Sacramento, California, was the top-giving church.

In 1994, Missionaries Bill and Kim Snider coupled one-minute radio messages with follow-up LFTL literature distribution to reach a remote area of the northern Philippines. In three towns, rallies were held after being announced on the air and in flyers. By the third week, the crowd was over 1,500 each night in one of the remote villages, even though the missionary group was harassed by bandits and followed by rebel militant groups. Hundreds were led to Christ and 30 Bible study groups were begun after the campaign.

One of the primary reasons for greatly increased LFTL giving in the 1990s was well-organized spring and fall tours in Assemblies of God districts. In Oregon, for example, two banquets were held in the district each night for several weeks in the fall. New York-cut steaks, potatoes, and all the trimmings drew church members to hear the LFTL story. Outstanding speakers and the 17-minute film, *The LFTL Story*, portrayed the critical need to provide more gospel literature to assist Assemblies of God missions efforts around the world.

Steak teams crisscrossed Arkansas. Nearly 2,000 people attended sectional banquets. A pastor at a small-town church in a building program felt prompted by the Holy Spirit to pledge $1,200 to LFTL. He took blank posters back to his congregation and shared the need for missions literature. His people responded by pledging over $2,700.

Spotlight, the bimonthly LFTL publication, contained testimonials from missionaries whose work had been assisted by LFTL. Over two tons of evangelistic material was distributed in Cameroon by Jim and Cynthia Lemons, the only Assemblies of God missionaries in that country. Karen Wuertz, missionary to Cambodia, wrote, "Thanks to the faithful councilmen of LFTL, New Testaments in Khmer translation have reached us. You should have seen the joy and surprise in the eyes of the girls in my Bible study when they received a Bible in their own language. Only eternity will tell how many thousands of lives have been touched and claimed for the Kingdom of God because of LFTL literature."

In 1994, the first Bibles ever in the Uzbek language were printed with LFTL funds and distributed to new converts in the Central Asian country of Uzbekistan. Missionary Del Kingsriter said, "It was one of the greatest thrills in my life. When Muslims responded and came forward for salvation, I was able to hand them a copy of the Bible they could read and understand. This was a powerful moment as I realized the teamwork that went into the production, purchase, and distribution of this literature."

LFTL went international in 1994 when Malaysia established its own program. Benny Ferguson and Don Jacques shared the LFTL vision with 100 men at a banquet in Kuala Lumpur, Malaysia's capital. At the close of the evening, Malaysian men pulled posters from the walls and made pledges of over 50,000 Malaysian dollars.

Money raised at this and other banquets in Malaysia was set aside for a Malaysian-led 1995 Prayer Task Force/Good News Crusade in Tanzania, East Africa.

Twenty-nine Assemblies of God districts conducted fall LFTL tours in 1994. A steak team from Tulsa, Oklahoma, and Benny Ferguson took the LFTL message to the campus of Southwestern Assemblies of God College (SAGC) in Waxahachie, Texas. SAGC President Delmer Guynes remembered his first LFTL experience 30 years before. Guynes wrote in *Spotlight,* "As a missionary in Malaysia, we received $15,000 to print enough literature to blanket the entire city of Kuala Lumpur and surrounding areas. In two months, we used Bible school students and people from the local church to saturate the area with tracts and other literature. At that time, there was only one church in the capital city. Today there are more than 50 strong churches in the area covered by that first LFTL crusade."

> *We must go forth to gather in the harvest for soon our Lord will come to earth again. And it's up to us to bring the lost to Him.*
>
> —FROM THE HYMN BY RANDY WRIGHT

twelve

At Home and Abroad

STORIES OF SALVATION AND LIVES CHANGED by introduction to Christ through LFTL literature continued to stream into LFTL headquarters in Springfield. Each year, a larger portion of the LFTL budget was allocated for the Assemblies of God home missions program, headed by Charles Hackett. More than $300,000 was budgeted for printing home missions literature in 1994 from contributions received for that specific purpose.

More than 100,000 copies of a special edition of the *Book of Hope*, designed to reach the African-American communities of the inner city, were distributed as part of the Royal Rangers Inner-City project. The book addressed 14 critical issues that faced young people in America's inner cities. Renowned artist Franklin M. Norfleet produced a special cover for the book.

The *Book of Hope* for urban missions went to Minnesota, Wisconsin, Rhode Island, and New Orleans, Louisiana, where home missionaries on the street distributed copies of the book during Mardi Gras. Mark Gregori received 10,000 copies for his work in high-rise apartments around his church in the Bronx, New York. The book was made available to 112 urban Assemblies of God home missionaries in 24 districts throughout the country.

Teen Challenge centers across the nation benefited from LFTL literature. Teen Challenge of Southern California not only used the literature for their own students but distributed tracts and booklets into drug and gang-infested areas.

LFTL funds also provided copies of *The Pentecostal Evangel* for use in prison ministry in the United States. "Key Bearers" was a cooperative effort between LFTL and the magazine to provide free *Evangels* to prisoners across the nation. In the second year of the program, 1,768 salvation reports were received.

Stacey Smith was a young woman who picked up a copy of *The Evangel* in a county jail. It changed her life. She wrote, "Even though I live in the United States, I had never heard about what Jesus could do for me. After reading the magazine, I remember thinking, *if I ever do follow Jesus, I want to belong to that church the magazine spoke of.*" Three days later, Stacey gave her heart to the Lord. Even while serving her prison sentence in Tucker Prison in Arkansas, Stacey wanted to become a member of a local Assemblies of God church. Pastor Randy Long of The Church Alive in Conway, Arkansas, asked his board members to approve Stacey's membership. They did.

Stacey began carrying the gospel to her fellow inmates. Healings and salvations were reported weekly. One guard received the Holy Spirit while attending a prison service. Chaplain Bob Holyfield said, "We should never underestimate what the Lord can do with a magazine."

One of the most unusual success stories of LFTL came in 1994 from Missionary Wayne Cagle, area director for Pacific Oceania. He told of a man in California who floated gospel tracts and booklets inside bottles. One floated to a province in the

A poster used to raise funds for printing the Book of Hope *in English and many other languages of the world. Laymen attending Light for the Lost banquets were asked to choose a project by literally removing a poster from the walls of the banquet meeting room. Courtesy LFTL.*

far Eastern Solomon Islands. The note inside the bottle promised a free Bible in exchange for names and addresses of people in his area who wanted to enroll in a Bible correspondence course.

The islander who found the bottle somehow scraped up enough money for a postage stamp and sent for his free Bible, along with 50 names of his neighbors. All 50 were sent the first lesson of *The Great Questions of Life.*

LEFT: *John Bueno, Latin American field director for the Division of Foreign Missions of the Assemblies of God, spoke to councilmen at the 1994 national convention. Bueno later became executive director of the Division of Foreign Missions.*

RIGHT: *Charles Hackett, Assemblies of God Homes Missions director, thanked Light for the Lost councilmen at the 1994 convention for dedicating funds to reach the lost in America's inner cities.*

Eventually, the lessons were returned with thank you notes and a list of 32 more people wanting literature. From the 82 people, more than 300 courses were sent into the remote area that probably would have never seen a missionary.

Don Jacques, right, presents an honorary Light for the Lost councilman pin to Assemblies of God General Superintendent Thomas Trask in 1994.

give me the book!

Since its founding in 1969, Eurasia Teen Challenge (ETC) has been blessed by LFTL literature. Longtime ETC Director Al Perna, Jr., said, "LFTL funds made possible the distribution of literature in coffee houses and in street campaigns throughout Western and Eastern Europe." Copies of David Wilkerson's *The Cross and the Switchblade* went into jails with many testimonies of conversion. Teen Challenge field evangelist David "Pachie" Hamilton, a converted Irish gang member, used LFTL literature in crusades from Ireland to Holland to Romania.

LFTL funds helped launch the Teen Challenge Curriculum for evangelism and discipleship training as well as the *Turning Point* materials which have been translated into ten languages and accepted as educational material by many non-Christian governments in Europe.

The files of Gary Davidson, a missionary to Ireland since 1980, are filled with stories of men and women whose lives have been transformed because of the power of LFTL literature. Davidson recalled the story of a young man named Luke who was too bashful to approach an outreach team handing out cups of tea and hot soup, and a LFTL tract, on the streets of Dublin. However, a tract dropped by a disinterested passerby landed at Luke's feet. It told the story of John Edwards whose life of addiction had been changed because of an encounter with Christ.

The tract included an invitation to St. Mark's Church in Dublin. The following Sunday, Luke found himself standing outside the church, unable to overcome his low self esteem and depression and go inside. Finally, after several weeks, he followed a group into the church and sat in the back. At the close of the service, he responded to the call of the Holy Spirit, met the Lord, and was gloriously transformed. Luke now is part of the St. Mark's congregation, assists in the publication of the church's monthly newsletter, and plays the violin for worship service.

"Thanks to LFTL literature," Davidson said, "There are countless similar testimonies. I often meet visitors who show up at our church clutching a LFTL tract in their hand."

LEFT: *Members of First Assembly of God in Clarksville, Tennessee, remove posters off the wall at a March 1994, Light for the Lost banquet. The posters were used successfully to encourage pledges after LFTL banquets and rallies.*

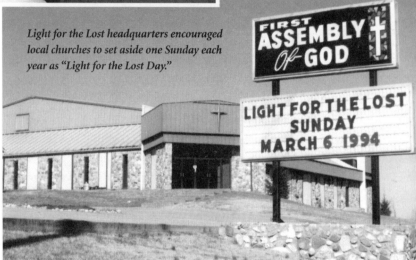

Light for the Lost headquarters encouraged local churches to set aside one Sunday each year as "Light for the Lost Day."

LFTL established two endowment funds in 1994 to guarantee LFTL giving in the future. The first allowed a councilman to set up an endowment to pay his dues for his lifetime and beyond. The second was a literature endowment fund through which individuals could donate property, receive substantial tax benefits, enjoy income for a lifetime, and establish a perpetual gift for the LFTL literature fund.

Annual sectional tours continued to be the major fund-raising activity of LFTL. In Oklahoma, Chuck Freeman coordinated rallies and banquets in which Gary Davidson, Southern Asia Missionary David Grant, Peninsular Asia Missionary Ron Maddux, and Rob Hoskins of Life Publishers spoke to audiences of more than 3,000 people. Those attending the banquets enjoyed a 12-ounce rib-eye steak, baked potato, and all the trimmings.

In Oregon, Benny Ferguson, Chuck Freeman, Missionary David Godwin, and Oklahoma City Pastor Colen Lassiter preached banquets and rallies in which goals were exceeded. The Prime Time Live presentation was made to explain the importance of councilmen and evangelism literature.

Even smaller districts were excited about LFTL. In South Dakota, District Men's Director Dwayne Pederson reported that even though half of the 50 churches in the district were home missions churches, every congregation made a commitment to LFTL.

More than 600 junior LFTL councilmen were added in 1994. More funds were raised to provide inner city home missions programs with copies of the *Book of Hope* for distribution. Don Jacques brought in one of his cook teams to do barbecued ribs at a LFTL Junior Councilman banquet. LFTL pledged support for the printing of *Edward Elephant Says,* an evangelistic comic book that tells how to keep from getting AIDS, how to help someone who has AIDS, and how to accept Jesus as Lord and Savior. Developed first for Africa, the comic book was also used in Latin America and in Thailand.

Edward Elephant Says, printed with Light for the Lost funds, was a unique tool to educate people about AIDS and to lead them to eternal life through a relationship with Jesus Christ. Courtesy LFTL.

Fayette Miller was honored as Councilman-of-the-Year in 1995. Miller, left, was presented his plaque by Assemblies of God Assistant General Superintendent Charles Crabtree. Since his days as a local pastor, Crabtree has been an avid supporter of Light for the Lost.

Several Oklahoma pastors went on a missions trip with Freeman in 1994 to distribute the *Book of Life* in Romania. Pastor Ron Meador of Duncan, Oklahoma, wrote, "My trip to Drobeta, Romania, was the fulfillment of a lifelong dream. There seems to be an innocence about the people. They are open...open to whoever gets there first."

The former Soviet Union was a fertile field for LFTL literature. Missionary Steven Puffpaff reported, "There is a hunger in Russia to know God. I recently joined a team going into the city of Smolensk, southwest of Moscow, to distribute the *Book of Life*. Each day we went into schools and handed a copy of the book to children who had been raised as atheists. You should have seen their faces as they opened the book and read about the precious life of Jesus Christ."

The annual LFTL convention returned to its roots in southern California in 1995, meeting at the Hyatt Regency Hotel in Irvine. Glen Cole, senior pastor of Sacramento's Capital Christian Center; Benny Ferguson; Missionary to Malawi

Southern California District Superintendent Ray Rachels receives the District-of-the-Year Award from Charles Crabtree at the 1995 national LFTL convention. Southern California topped the nation in LFTL giving.

ABOVE: *Missionary Bernhard Johnson was memorialized at the 1995 national convention. His widow, Doris Johnson, left, recognizing that her husband had held 225 mass crusades that recorded nearly two million converts, said, "Because of the faithful giving of LFTL councilmen, we were able to blanket capital cities, major metropolises, small towns, and villages with gospel packets." Sam and Geri assisted in the service honoring the Johnsons.*

RIGHT: *At the Gold Key Breakfast at the annual Light for the Lost convention in 1995, Assemblies of God Foreign Missions Executive Director Loren Triplett presented his formula for the world's greatest revival. Two hundred sixty one LFTL councilmen earned their diamond key pin in the previous year.*

at home and abroad

ABOVE: *Sam with special foreign guests at the 1995 national convention.*

BELOW: *The national Light for the Lost executive committee in 1995. Left to right, Terry Raburn, Assemblies of God director of Church Ministries, Jerry Freeman, Don Jacques, Benny Ferguson, Otto Wegner, Joe Livesay, and Len Ventling.*

RIGHT: *Assemblies of God General Secretary George Wood, left, presents the 1995 Church-of-the-Year Award to Glen Cole, pastor of Capital Christian Center in Sacramento, California. Cole's church led the nation's local congregations in giving to LFTL.*

ABOVE: *Prayer is always a key ingredient of any national Light for the Lost convention, banquet, or rally. Here, men at the 1995 convention ask God's blessing on the opening session.*

Two of the early Light for the Lost councilmen addressed the 1995 national convention. Hollis Lawson, left, was at the altar at First Assembly of God in Santa Ana, California, the night in 1952 when God gave Sam the vision that became Light for the Lost. Ray Neill, right, was one of Sam's earliest supporters. He caught Sam's vision, and as God blessed his business, promoted Light for the Lost worldwide.

Dean Galyen; and Assemblies of God General Superintendent Thomas Trask were featured speakers for the convention.

Latin American Field Director John Bueno and Division of Foreign Missions Director Loren Triplett paid tribute during the convention to Missionary-Evangelist Bernhard Johnson who died in February 1995. Sam and Geri presented Johnson's widow, Doris, with a dozen roses as part of the tribute.

In Johnson's last missionary report, the legendary South American missionary still sang the praises of LFTL. After 3,000 believers distributed 300,000 pieces of LFTL literature during a crusade in Cuiaba, in western Brazil, Johnson wrote, "I gave an altar call on the closing night of the crusade to 40,000 people. Nearly 2,000 were saved. They would never have been reached without LFTL literature. LFTL is vital to mass crusades."

Councilman-of-the-Year at the 1995 convention was Dennis Wolf of Wisconsin. Pastor-of-the-Year was Jerry Brooks of Oak Creek Assembly in Oak Creek, Wisconsin. Indiana District Superintendent Charles Crank won the Superintendent-of-the-Year Award. Indiana had the highest average-per-church giving of $1,113.59. The Southern California District was again tops in district LFTL giving, with $390,309 for 1994. Capital Christian Center was honored as the nation's top giving LFTL church. The Sacramento, California, church gave $62,565. Woodlake Assembly of God in Tulsa, Oklahoma, was second, at $52,294 in LFTL offerings.

Sam was honored for his lifetime of work for LFTL at the Assemblies of God General Council in 1995. General Superintendent Thomas Trask presented Sam with the Superintendent's Medal of Honor, the fellowship's highest award

National Vice President Jerry Freeman tries on a new "cook" hat. Freeman was a second generation Light for the Lost national officer. His father is Chuck Freeman.

for a layman, for "an exemplary life, bringing honor to God and His church."

After the presentation, Sam received dozens of letters of congratulations. Southern California District Superintendent Ray Rachels wrote, "You have given wonderful, outstanding years of ministry and service to the Lord's Kingdom...Your faithfulness, love for the church, concern for people, and willingness to always go the second mile are a model for us all."

Assemblies of God General Secretary George O. Wood, said, "There never has been a more deserving recipient of the Medal of Honor." Benny Ferguson wrote, "I will always be eternally grateful for the fact that you were obedient to the vision God gave you. A multitude of souls will be in heaven because you did something with the vision given to you by our Lord."

The LFTL office not only received thousands of good news reports about the fruits of literature distribution, but also heard from councilmen whose lives had been changed for just participating in the program. After Benny Ferguson spoke at a LFTL emphasis service at Calvary Temple in Springfield, a new councilman wrote, "I felt led to become a coun-

The Superintendent's Medal of Honor hangs around Sam's neck. The highest award for an Assemblies of God layman was given Sam at the 1995 General Council.

cilman. We had already set our family missions budget for the year but I could see the potential for saving thousands of souls for only 50 cents a day. I became a councilman that morning. The following

ABOVE: *Assemblies of God General Superintendent G. Raymond Carlson, right, presents Sam with a Gold Key Award.*

Wednesday I was unexpectedly informed that starting the next day, I would receive a 50 cents per hour raise in pay!"

Mike McGee, a missionary-in-residence at North Central Bible College (NCBC), accompanied a NCBC group to Guadalajara, Mexico, in 1995, to a city in which he previously had served as an Assemblies of God missionary. The team took the gospel to 13 cities in Mexico. LFTL literature was handed out in town squares and marketplaces. Hundreds of children and adults opened their hearts to Christ.

In September 1995, a LFTL Prayer Task Force team invaded the countries of Poland and Hungary. For ten days, councilmen traveled throughout the countryside, praying for the establishment of churches in unreached areas.

Fall continued to be the busiest season for LFTL banquets. In late 1995, eight districts reported to headquarters with amazing stories. In Arkansas, five different speakers shared the need for literature with 1,700 people in 16 banquets to raise $208,000 in literature pledges and enroll 34 councilmen. Missionaries to Latin America David Thomas and Jimmy Susa helped raise record pledges at banquets in Kentucky. In Montana, Oklahoma, Oregon, and in the Rocky Mountain and

RIGHT: *The cover of the special edition of* The Pentecostal Evangel *funded by* Light for the Lost *in 1995. Courtesy* The Pentecostal Evangel.

PENTECOSTAL Evangel

NOT BY MIGHT, NOR BY POWER, BUT BY MY SPIRIT, SAITH THE LORD

DAVID ROBINSON: JAMMIN' AGAINST THE DARKNESS

Steve Jamison and NBA players take a stand

ABOVE: *Light for the Lost dollars were used to publish a special undated edition of* The Pentecostal Evangel *in the summer of 1995. Featuring a cover photograph of National Basketball Association star David Robinson, the outreach edition was designed "to attract a broad audience that has yet to hear the message of salvation." In this photograph, Assemblies of God officials pray over a shipment of the special edition of the* Evangel. *Left to right, Efraim Espinoza of the Decade of Harvest office;* Evangel *Editor Hal Donaldson; Assemblies of God General Superintendent Thomas Trask; and Benny Ferguson, national LFTL coordinator. Courtesy* The Pentecostal Evangel.

*The Oklahoma District was first in total LFTL giving in 1996. The 500
Assemblies of God churches in Oklahoma contributed $386,205. Chuck
Freeman passed the 250 mark in councilmen enrolled during his 30 years in
LFTL work and was honored for the achievement. Accepting the top-giving
award for Oklahoma were left to right, Chuck Freeman, Oklahoma District
Superintendent Armon Newburn, District Men's Ministries Director Lindell
Warren, and Jerry Freeman.*

Pennsylvania-Delaware Districts, volunteers took the message
to banquets and rallies.

LFTL councilmen joined forces with Chi Alpha, the
Assemblies of God college and university campus outreach program, in a unique partnership at the biggest football game in
Oklahoma in 1995. LFTL Vice President Jerry Freeman and
Oklahoma Chi Alpha Coordinator Greg Tiffany promoted the
tailgate party before the annual Oklahoma University-Oklahoma
State University football game. The barbecued rib feast and open-
air gospel concert drew more than 1,200 youth. Sales from the ribs
raised over $8,000 that day for campus outreach.

In 1996, Prayer Task Force trips were made to Tegucigalpa,
Honduras; Budapest, Hungary; Ulan Bator, Mongolia; and Bissau,

Otto Wegner of Wisconsin served as national president of Light for the Lost from 1996 to 2000. He formerly was national vice president.

Guinea-Bissau. LFTL councilmen paid their own expenses to travel to foreign soil to pray over national pastors and outreach centers. They also distributed tons of LFTL literature.

The theme of the 1996 annual LFTL convention was "Jesus…the Light." At the convention in Springfield, Assemblies of God Missions Field Director for Africa, Don Corbin, challenged councilmen with using the "Three R's" in missions, "writing, reading, and running with the vision."

Outgoing National President Don Jacques preached a powerful message about the joy of seeing the lost saved. Other convention speakers were Bob Houlihan, field director for Asia Pacific; Missionary Gary Davidson; Jerry

Mark Burke of North Dakota was elected national vice president at the 1996 national Light for the Lost convention.

Parsley, field director for Eurasia; and John Bueno, field director for Latin America.

Otto Wegner was elected the new national LFTL president. Jerry Freeman charmed the Friday night banquet with his latest "top ten list." John Thompson from Indiana was Councilman-of-the-Year with 23 new councilmen enrolled. Mike Purkey of Lenexa Christian Center in Kansas City, Kansas, was again Pastor-of-the-Year. Charles Crank repeated as District Superintendent-of-the-Year as Indiana led the nation in per-church giving at $1,358.14. First Assembly in Lafayette, Indiana, was the country's top giving church with offerings of $57,948, followed by Capital Christian Center in Sacramento, California, at $54,961.

> *Let us not grow weary in the work of love, Send the light! Send the light! Let us gather jewels for a crown above, Send the light! Send the light!*
>
> —FROM THE TRADITIONAL HYMN BY CHARLES GABRIEL

thirteen

Prayer Changes Things

WHEN THE MEMBERSHIP OF LFTL WAS OPENED to ministers, Del Kingsriter was one of the first to stand in line to become a councilman. As director of the Center for Ministry to Muslims, Kingsriter believed that there is a direct correlation between the growth of LFTL and the growth of overseas membership in the Assemblies of God. He said, "When we first started as missionaries, before LFTL, it was tough sledding. If I could take a graph and chart the growth of converts, I know it would parallel the growth of the LFTL."

LFTL was a vital component of the Assemblies of God outreach during the 1996 Olympics in Atlanta, Georgia. Seventeen Assemblies of God districts participated. An example was the Michigan District AIM team, with more than 300 members, that distributed 250,000 pieces of literature. More than a million copies of a special Olympics outreach edition of *The Pentecostal Evangel* were also distributed.

The Arkansas Light for the Lost steak team prepares for a large crowd during the fall tour. Courtesy LFTL.

In December 1996, nine LFTL councilmen from Oklahoma and Arkansas left for India on what they thought was "just another Prayer Task Force trip." Wayne Long remembered, "Time seemed to fly as we prayed with the national pastors six to eight hours a day."

However, a single convert won to the Lord during a Sunday night service may have impacted the lives of thousands of Indian children. The convert was a monk who was in charge of the public schools in the sprawling city of New Delhi. Team member Jerry Freeman recalled, "It did not take *Book of Life* publisher Bob Hoskins very long to figure out that through the new convert, he could give each student in New Delhi a copy of the *Book of Life*." Freeman said, "God moves where there seems to be no way!"

"Slam Dunk AIDS" was the unique title of a LFTL tract that rolled off the printing presses in 1997. In the tract sports hero, Slam Dunk, presented the facts about AIDS awareness and prevention in a clear and concise manner. The tract not only educates youth, it introduces them to Jesus Christ.

LFTL also underwrote the printing of soul-winning material for the Chi Alpha, Chaplaincy, Intercultural Ministries, MAPS/RV, New Church Evangelism, and Teen Challenge programs of the Assemblies of God.

"The Joy of Serving the Lord as a Councilman," was the title of a special article written by Don Jacques in the January-February 1997 edition of *Spotlight.* Jacques wrote:

> Councilmen, let us lay aside every weight, let us run the race, and let us look unto Jesus. Our race is producing enough money to give our missionaries the ability to tell the whole world about Christ's love…What is the joy set before a LFTL council-man that will make him endure self denial and go for the gold? Is it the joy of cooking the best steak in the world? No. The joy of traveling around the district or the country? No. The joy of fellowshipping with other LFTL men? No. The joy of diamond keys earned? No. All of these are good, but Luke 15 says "…joy shall be in heaven over one sinner that repenteth…" Let us get close enough to Christ that

Pastor Steve Dow of First Assembly of God, Topeka, Kansas, left, receives a special recognition award in 1997 from Assemblies of God General Treasurer James Bridges.

the joy that motivated Him to endure the cross becomes fulfilled in us and becomes the prize that motivates us to excellence in our endeavors.

The 1997 LFTL annual convention was held in Indianapolis, Indiana. Speakers included Benny Ferguson, Central American Missions Outreach Director Doug Peterson, Assemblies of God General Treasurer James Bridges, Northern Missouri District Superintendent Manuel Shoults, and Colen Lassiter, pastor of the Rock Assembly of God in Oklahoma City.

Two of the three laypersons honored at the 47th General Council of the Assemblies of God in Indianapolis in 1997 were LFTL councilmen. Ray Neill and Chuck Freeman received the Superintendent's Medal of Honor.

Neill, founder and builder of the Neill Aircraft Company in Long Beach, California, has been involved with LFTL since 1958. He and his wife, Geneva, financed the building of 15 Assemblies of God churches overseas and make frequent trips to encourage and assist missionaries through coordinating Good News Crusades and distributing LFTL literature. The Neills attend First Assembly in Wilmington, California.

Freeman pioneered LFTL in Oklahoma, the district that led the nation in giving in

Assemblies of God General Superintendent Thomas Trask presents the fellowship's highest layman award, the Superintendent's Medal of Honor, to Ray Neill, above, and Chuck Freeman, left, at General Council in 1997. Courtesy The Pentecostal Evangel.

1995 and 1996. He organized the first Prayer Task Force team to Mexico in 1979. By 1997, he had taken 17 teams to countries around the globe. He and his wife, Inez, attend Capitol Hill Assembly of God in Oklahoma City.

On a trip to Zambia, Missionary Bill Moore was visiting the parliament buildings in the capital city of Lusaka. In one such building, used as a library for members of the Zambia parliament, a library clerk hinted that the library was always looking for books. Prompted by the Holy Spirit, Moore asked if he could provide

Sam and Geri and their children, left to right, Ron, Gary, Sue, and Jim.

copies of the *Full Life Study Bible* (FLSB) for the library. Notes for the FLSB, the first widely distributed and highly regarded study Bible for Pentecostal believers, were written by Assemblies of God Missionary Don Stamps. Moore remembered, "The clerk practically begged me to get copies of the Bible."

Moore was able to gather 17 copies of the *Full Life Study Bible,* each inscribed with the words, "Presented to the Zambia Parliament by the men of the Assemblies of God, USA–Light for the Lost."

In 1997, LFTL became partners in evangelism with the National Youth Department of the Assemblies of God. The Youth Department's vision was to reach every unsaved student in America's public schools. LFTL provided money for the printing of the *Book of Hope* for use in the Campus Missions program. LFTL officials committed to put the *Book of Hope* into a packet available for every campus missionary. The copy was intended to be a reference point for student missionaries, introducing them to a powerful witnessing tool. Student Missions Field Representative Tom Greene said, "I see Campus Missions and the *Book of Hope* as a tremendous opportunity to increase the vision of LFTL as we continue to provide literature to missionaries around the world."

A new literature tool, a coloring book and AIDS prevention comic book, "Danny Dolphin," was produced in 1997, an offshoot of the "Edward Elephant" Aids prevention comic booklet. The artwork for the Pacific version was completed in Guam. Seventy five thousand copies were distributed in Saipan, Palau, the Marshall Islands, Pohnpei, Fiji, Tonga, Vanuatu, the Cook Islands, and the Solomon Islands.

In 1997, Sam and Geri celebrated their golden wedding anniversary. The entire Cochran clan gathered to honor their parents and grandparents.

"God's Word in tract form is sharper than a two-edged sword," wrote Missionary to Spain, Daniel West in 1997. West related the story of an evangelistic crusade in a park in the city of Sevilla. A young man was given a tract. As he read it, he felt urged to stay and listen to the songs and testimonies. After one of the students preached, there were tears in his eyes. The following morning, he attended an Assemblies of God church and committed his life to Christ.

Twenty-eight tent crusades were held throughout Hungary in the summer of 1997. Each local church received thousands of copies of the LFTL-funded gospel tract *Meghivo*, the Hungarian word for "invitation." Nearly 20,000 people attended the crusades. Each received a LFTL packet of information instructing them how to accept Christ and how to get in touch with a local Assemblies of God fellowship.

LFTL underwrote the cost of many translations of comic books for use by missionaries and evangelists on foreign soil. ICI University, now known as Global University, printed a series of comics portraying the lives and ministries of key Bible characters. In 1998, Jerry and Faith McCollough, missionaries to the Slovak Republic, reported that the comics "Gideon," "David," and "Esther" were a vital part of their summer evangelistic crusades among Slovakian young people.

"Edward the Elephant Says Help Stop AIDS," the comic developed by Missionary Don Tucker as a powerful tool against the spread of AIDS, was translated into a dozen languages. By 1999, more than 12 million copies had been distributed in the areas of the world hit hardest by the AIDS epidemic.

As the 20th century came to a close, a visit to Cuba by Pope John Paul II actually created an atmosphere of growing religious freedom in the Communist island nation, allowing evangelical Christians to hold public rallies.

LFTL provided tons of tracts and other gospel literature to be distributed during celebrations in the summer of 1999. The Cuban

Bible Society printed 500,000 Bibles. The government-approved "Cuban Evangelical Celebration" consisted of open-air gatherings in a dozen cities across Cuba. Five thousand copies of the *Full Life Study Bible* were given to local pastors and church leaders.

Richard Nicholson, regional director of Latin America and the Caribbean for the Assemblies of God Division of Foreign Missions, described one revival that had broken out in Cuba:

> As the church in Madruga gained a reputation for experiencing God's presence, crowds started coming from across the nation. Trains filled with people unloaded at the local depot and a steady stream of visitors walked to the church. For eight months they had services from 8 a.m. to midnight, every day. This was a place with no air conditioning and no fans. Two hundred people would be packed inside. Another 200 stood outside and another 200 sat on a terrace. People waited to be cycled into services every 90 minutes. They literally soaked the floor with perspiration.

Missionaries in other parts of the world cried out for help to fund literature distribution programs. At the 1999 national LFTL convention in Charlotte, North Carolina, Greg Mundis, Assemblies of God missions Europe director, presented the urgent needs of refugees fleeing Yugoslavia. Mundis said the refugees were destitute, afraid, and in need of hope for the future. He said, "We see an immediate opportunity to be able to minister to the whole person."

LFTL councilmen responded with offerings and pledges of $100,000 for literature to take the gospel to the Yugoslav refugees.

After a 1999 forest fire scorched more than 5,000 acres of land and destroyed 30 buildings on an Indian reservation in northeast Arizona, the White Mountain Apache Tribe asked Whiteriver Assembly of God to be the main distribution point for emergency food and clothing.

Every bag of supplies contained a copy of "The Last Best Thing," printed using funds raised by LFTL junior councilmen. This special edition of the Book of John included a preface that discussed life issues and included the plan of salvation. More than 7,000 copies of the book were distributed through the fire-relief effort. As a result, at least eight people were saved and new families were added to the local church.

Gary Crump, working with missionaries Don and Terri Triplett in their King's Castle ministry in El Salvador, explained the awesome power of literature, especially in Latin America. Crump wrote, "If tracts were distributed to schoolchildren or in a public park in the United States, as many as half of them would wind up on the ground or in the nearest garbage can. In comparison, a tract placed in the hand of anyone in Central America is considered a gift. In this culture a gift is taken home, to be shared with all the family members and neighbors."

Crump said that in six years, he personally had handed out 25,000 tracts and had seen only two left on the street. One had fallen into a mud puddle and was irretrievable for the little girl who stood there crying until she was given another tract. The other one was eaten by a chicken that was quicker than the little boy who tried his best to rescue it.

The "permanency" of the message of a LFTL tract was graphically described by Crump:

> Often, as we disembark from a Castle bus to begin inviting the children to a street crusade, a child will run up to us with a dingy, well-used tract that he received in a previous visit by a Castle team. Only eternity knows how many times the brightly colored pages have been turned, making it ragged and brown with use. How many souls have been introduced to the love of God as demonstrated through the gift of His Son Jesus by reading its simple message?

In the final year of the millennium, more than $10.5 million was raised through LFTL to provide literature for Assemblies of God missionaries, an increase of $2.5 million over the previous year. A total of 3,462 churches made LFTL contributions.

Councilmen income reached a record $1.26 million for administration. More than three thousand new councilmen were added, bringing the active list to 9,290. In its first 48 years, LFTL had raised nearly $90 million for missions literature.

The Oklahoma District swept the top giving awards for 1999. Lakeside Assembly of God in Oklahoma City gave $2,019,599, and received the Church-of-the-Year Award. In second place, giving $93,912, was Woodlake Assembly of God in Tulsa. The third place award went to Weatherford Assembly of God. The pastor of the church in Weatherford, a small city in western Oklahoma, enjoyed a rich LFTL heritage. Ric Freeman's father was former National President Chuck Freeman. His brother, Jerry, served as national vice president.

Oklahoma received the District-of-the-Year Award and Armon Newburn was presented the District Superintendent-of-the-Year Award.

Dale Applegate of LaPorte, Indiana, enrolled 86 new councilmen, winning the Councilman-of-the-Year Award. The Pastor-of-the-Year Award, given annually to the pastor of the church with the most new councilmen, went to Cardenio Montoya of Clarksville, Tennessee, with 78 new councilmen enrolled at First Assembly of God.

Don Jacques was elected national president for a third term. Jerry Freeman, Mark Burke, Loyd Hoskins, and Jerry Terry were elected as vice presidents.

Delegates to the 1999 LFTL convention approved a resolution to designate the *Full Life Study Bible* as an acceptable evangelistic tool of LFTL. The FLSB had been found to be more than just a tool for teaching. Printed in 17 languages, the FLSB was an incredible tool of evangelism. The official designation allowed missionaries to use the study Bible without questioning whether it was evangelistic literature or not. Millions of copies of the FLSB were printed in Chinese with a green acrylic cover emblazoned with a flame. In China the FLSB is known as the "Fire Bible." A worker in China said the Fire Bible is the key to maintaining the thousands coming to Christ each month and the house churches that are springing up around China.

The worker said, "Maybe the Chinese don't even know how to preach, but they can read the Fire Bible. When they teach and preach, they can use the study notes. This is especially important for a country without seminars and other forms of pastoral training." One imprisoned pastor in China said, "Keep sending Fire Bibles until we say it's enough!"

With more than $10 million in contributions to LFTL programs and nearly 10,000 councilmen, LFTL National Coordinator Benny Ferguson told the 1999 annual convention:

TO GOD BE THE GLORY, GREAT THINGS HE HATH DONE!

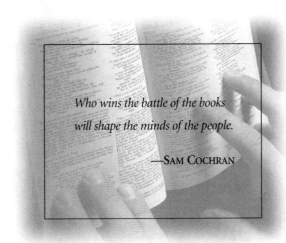

Who wins the battle of the books
will shape the minds of the people.

—SAM COCHRAN

fourteen

Pursue the Vision

FROM ITS HUMBLE BEGINNINGS nearly a half century before, Light for the Lost began the 21st century as a healthy and success-ful tool of evangelism, at home and in foreign lands. LFTL was responsive to pleas for help for the printed word to take the pre-cious story of Jesus Christ to the lost of the world.

New and fresh stories of how one piece of LFTL literature changed hundreds of lives were told. In Italy, Luigi Pollidori pas-tored a church of 300 and was in the process of mothering two other churches, all because he and his wife accepted the Lord 30 years before when they read a LFTL gospel tract and sent for "The Great Questions of Life" correspondence course. Because the Pollidoris lived over 200 miles from the closest evangelical church, they started their own. In three decades, hundreds of Italians have made a decision for Christ, a direct result of the one gospel tract.

In 2000, Light for the Lost designated funds for the publication of a series of "PowerMark" comic books developed by Steve Benintendi. The books used ancient and futuristic action characters to lead young minds to Jesus Christ. Courtesy PowerMark Productions.

Fire Bibles needed in China

The church in China has been experiencing "one of the most spectacular awakenings in Asian history," reports Aaron Rothganger, a worker in China. Thousands are coming to Christ, and new house churches are springing up across the country.

Rothganger says the "Fire Bible" (the Full Life Study Bible translated into Chinese) is crucial to this process. When a person becomes a church leader, the most essential thing to have is a Bible.

"Maybe they don't even know how to teach, but they can read the Bible," Rothganger said.

"When they teach and preach, they can use the study notes."

This is especially important for a country without seminaries or other forms of pastoral training.

"That's all the teaching [and] feeding those people . . . are getting."

Light for the Lost is committed to continued support for this exciting project.

"Keep sending Fire Bibles until we say it's enough."
— *an imprisoned pastor in China*

—300-400 baptisms and 30 new churches per month in just one city.
—To give one Bible to each current church leader means giving 14,000 in one network in one city.
—Only $8 to print a Bible. You can help!

see other side ⟶

This Light for the Lost brochure solicits funds for the Chinese-language Full Life Study Bibles. The so-called "Fire Bible" provides Pentecostal study notes for leaders of the hundreds of churches in China. LFTL, through Life Publishers, needed $8 to print and distribute a Fire Bible. Courtesy LFTL.

Sam and Geri Cochran, 1998.

Evangelist Jim King reported the testimony of Victor Tsarev in the Ukraine who had decided in early 2000 to take his own life. Addicted to narcotics, Victor saw no way out until one morning, on his way to buy drugs, he spotted a *Book of Hope* in a shady area near an apartment building. He took the book home and read it many times. He recalled, "Hope began to rise up within me and I began to turn to God." The young man gave his life to Christ and was completely set free from narcotics addition.

For the second year in a row, Sam was unable to attend the annual LFTL convention in Portland, Oregon, in April 2001. Back surgery forced him to a rehabilitation center near his home in California. Ill health had also stricken Geri.

But Sam was definitely at the convention in spirit. After all, it was his vision, his dream, his sweat and hard work that helped make LFTL one of the most daring and fruitful evangelical efforts since Paul and the other apostles carried the word of the risen Savior to their world in the first century.

At the 2001 national convention, with the theme of "Pursue the Vision," Lakeside Assembly in Oklahoma City, Oklahoma, was honored as the Church-of-the-Year with LFTL giving of $2,103,781. In second place was Woodlake Assembly in Tulsa, Oklahoma, with offerings of $97,200. The Assembly of God in Covina, California, finished third with $77,787.

LIGHT FOR THE LOST

EUROPE

Country or Missionary: Evangelism Literature Project

ONE OF SEVERAL MISSIONARIES SERVING AS TEAM MEMBERS

 # 1700
Project Number

Amount of Faith Promise

If project is over-funded, LFTL will direct your gift to another approved project.

*An effective way
to raise money following a Light for the Lost banquet
was for the speaker to encourage members of the audience to prayerfully
select a LFTL poster off the wall. This poster was used to raise money for
distribution of gospel literature in Europe. Courtesy LFTL.*

Oklahoma swept many of the awards at the 2001 national Light for the Lost convention in Portland, Oregon. Left to right, Michael Goldsmith, pastor of Broken Arrow Assembly of God, LFTL Pastor-of-the-Year; Oklahoma Men's Ministries Director Lindell Warren holds the District-of-the-Year Award; Oklahoma District Superintendent Frank Cargill won the Superintendent-of-the-Year Award; Pastor Ted Heaston of Woodlake Assembly of God in Tulsa, Oklahoma, second in national giving; Chuck Freeman holds the award for Lakeside Assembly of God in Oklahoma City, the top-giving church for the previous year. Courtesy Robert Burke.

The District-of-the-Year was again Oklahoma, with a phenomenal total of $7,245,173. The other top ten districts in LFTL total giving were Southern California, Southern Missouri, Illinois, Indiana, Arkansas, Northwest, Potomac, Wisconsin-Northern Michigan, and North Texas.

Councilman-of-the-Year was Warren Wilson of River of Life Assembly in Madison, Mississippi, who signed up 76 new councilmen the previous year. Wilson finished ahead of Bill Davis of First Assembly, La Mesa, California, and Steve Isaak of the Assembly of God in American Falls, Idaho. Jerry

Terry and Jerry Freeman were reelected as national LFTL vice presidents.

Pastor-of-the-Year for 2001 was Michael Goldsmith of Broken Arrow Assembly of God in Broken Arrow, Oklahoma, where 38 councilmen were added in 2000. LFTL Director-of-the-Year was Dwayne Pederson of South Dakota. The District Men's-Director-of-the-Year Award was presented to Jeff Mantz of South Dakota.

The Sam Cochran influence was felt at the Portland convention. Speakers gave reports on how he and Geri were faring physically. Also, Ron Cochran, Sam and Geri's son, directed the choir of Portland Christian Center that ministered during the Friday night banquet.

In 2001, every Assemblies of God district in the United States participated in LFTL. Also, money was received from LFTL groups in the Southern Pacific, Latin American, Spanish Eastern, Northern Pacific, Latin American, Central Latin American, German, Korean, and Puerto Rico Districts.

There were 9,753 LFTL councilmen, actively contributing $15 monthly to support the administration of the program. Oklahoma, with 1,436 councilmen, led the nation, followed by Southern California, Southern Missouri, Indiana, North Texas, and Wisconsin-Northern Michigan. North Dakota led the fellowship in averaging 3.23 councilmen per church in the district.

Longtime Light for the Lost councilman Bob Bruder at the 2001 national convention. Courtesy Robert Burke.

"The heart and soul of the ministry of LFTL," said John Bueno, executive director of the Assemblies of God Division of Foreign Missions, "is still the printed page." Bueno wrote, "The printed page needs no batteries; only someone who can read with an open heart."

WHAT'S THE FUTURE OF LFTL? That pertinent question was asked of many of the participants of the 2001 LFTL convention. Here are some of the responses:

> The future of LFTL is unlimited. Millions of lost souls are still untouched, so our job is not finished.
>
> —RAY NEILL

> Our job is still vital to missions. Our literature can go where missionaries cannot.
>
> —PHIL BRAUCHLER

> Our role will never, never end until Jesus comes. It's the Word of God we're delivering.
>
> —BOB BRUDER

> God will use LFTL as a major player in the final evangelization of the earth.
>
> —JOE LIVESAY

> We must enlist fresh leaders to create an appetite for younger Assemblies of God men to replace our old soldiers.
>
> —RAY RACHELS

> There is no limit to what can be accomplished.
>
> —BILL DAVIS

God has raised up a good army and it will continue to grow until our Lord returns.

—JERRY TERRY

We need national pastors to develop local and original materials in cultural context. We can win the whole world for Jesus.

—RON MADDUX

With more effort than ever before, we will see more giving and more results in saved souls, as long as we remain true to Sam Cochran's vision.

—ARNOLD NEWTON

We must work quickly and do more and more. Ours is a tremendous opportunity to fulfill the Great Commission.

—RALPH HILTON

As long as people read, we have a mission. We must do all we can until Jesus comes.

—DON JACQUES

The future is tremendous. With open fields, our potential is expanded.

—OTTO WEGNER

Assemblies of God General Superintendent Thomas Trask expressed the urgency of propagating the gospel. He wrote to LFTL councilmen, "Brethren, these are certainly the last days before our Lord's return and it is absolutely incumbent that we do

National Light for the Lost Coordinator Benny Ferguson and members of his staff at the 2001 national convention in Portland, Oregon. Left to right, Ferguson, Heather Scranton, Becky Harp, and Waketa Williams. Courtesy Robert Burke.

our best to hasten the Lord's return, for He said, 'this gospel of the kingdom will be preached in the whole world as a testimony to all nations, and then the end will come.'"

The challenge for Light for the Lost in the new millennium was framed by Assistant General Superintendent Charles Crabtree, who said, "The open doors in so many new countries make it impossible for us to sit back and be satisfied with yesterday."

Foreign Missions Director John Bueno said, "The Word of God is needed in print now more than ever before and is still an economic and effective way of reaching the lost with the gospel. I believe this will not diminish for many years to come. Our missionaries consider LFTL councilmen heroes, because they are the supply line that empowers them to distribute the gospel in printed form to many millions of people each year."

National LFTL Vice President Jerry Freeman wrote, "The 21st century is truly here. Wow! One hundred years ago no one would have dared to even dream about the opportunities to evangelize that we have today. Even the 'printed page' has taken on new meaning. With the press of a button we can literally 'send' the gospel anywhere in the world and print it in any language." Freeman asked, "Will we seize the opportunity?"

The *Full Life Study Bible* continued to play a major role in LFTL. By 2001, more than one million copies had been printed in nine languages. The FLSB was in production in 23 additional languages. According to Life Publishers Director, John Griffin, requests for the study Bible in 17 other languages were being considered.

LFTL provided funds to daily print tons of literature around the world for distribution by Assemblies of God missionaries and evangelists and national pastors. The Word of God never sleeps; nor do LFTL presses.

LFTL also teamed with Global University to provide gospel literature in 130 languages to the world's half billion Internet users. In most every country of the world, far from the touch of a human missionary, correspondence courses such as "The Great Questions of Life" were available for study online and immediate printing in the user's language.

Entry into the Internet world for LFTL was the result of a resolution passed at the 2001 national convention. For the first time ever, the scope of LFTL was expanded beyond traditional printed literature.

Benny Ferguson, national LFTL coordinator, said, "The future of LFTL is almost boundless. We are limited only by our humanity. Our assignment is not complete until every person on this earth has an opportunity to be saved."

That was Sam Cochran's vision in 1952. It remains the vision of the Assemblies of God and Light for the Lost in the 21st century.

In the words of the great hymn:

Harvest time, harvest time,
The Savior's calling, the grain is falling.
Oh, do not wait, it's growing late.
Behold the field is white,
It's harvest time.

WHAT CAN MEN DO FOR GOD?

(A story written by Sam Cochran and published in
The Pentecostal Evangel, February 9, 1986)

A printer developed movable type and used it to print the Bible.
A cobbler toiled long and hard to pay expenses to take the gospel of
Jesus Christ to a foreign land.

A man who designed an improved plow has blessed new
churches in the Assemblies of God through his stewardship.

There is no end to the wonderful stories of what men can do for
God.

WHY ARE MEN NEEDED TODAY?

Twelve ordinary men, first century disciples of Jesus, changed
the course of history through the power of the Holy Spirit. We can
accomplish comparable things for God today by His help.

Our nation is delinquent in its moral and religious responsi-
bilities. America needs stout-hearted men; men who will not
count their lives dear unto themselves; men of moral courage;
clean men; honest men; men of God.

DO MEN WANT TO SERVE?

Note the accounts of the early disciples' ministry. See how little description is given to their accomplishments compared to the works of Jesus Christ.

The pattern must be the same today. Jesus said, "I, if I be lifted up from the earth, will draw all men unto me"(John 12:32).

Most men are willing to serve. What they want are opportunities and direction.

Your motive must be to work as a faithful servant of Christ, not looking for approval from others.

WHERE CAN MEN SERVE?

First, your church has many departments where you can serve. Ushers provide a vital, needed service. The Sunday School needs teachers, department superintendents, welcoming committeemen, and others. The Men's Ministries group may need a Light for the Lost representative or assistance in Royal Rangers. Every church needs persons who will pray for and participate in outreach ministry.

The choir and orchestra need recruits. Men who can repair, paint, and keep the building in good condition are always in demand. Men are needed to visit newcomers, shut-ins, and prospects. Some churches need adults as sponsors for youth ministries. Volunteer to keep missionaries and evangelists in your home. You may personally support a missionary through your church.

Each district has places in which you may serve. Volunteers are needed to build home missions churches and to work at campgrounds. Youth camps need Christian counselors. The district Sunday School Department often needs workers.

National headquarters needs help and support. Make your occupational or professional services available there. You are needed to help finance and counsel with Assemblies of God colleges.

WHAT DOES IT COST TO SERVE?

In the world, the greater the position of service, the greater the cost. It is much the same in the service of the Lord. You must give leisure time, suffer inconveniences, and consecrate your finances before you can truly be effective for God.

I remember board meetings which lasted until 2 a.m. before a solution was found. I recall times when financial sacrifices were necessary to complete a project for the Lord.

Working with people of different views is necessary. Learn to accept graciously the decisions of those over you.

Each person is called to serve in a different capacity. Saul was king, an earthly office; Samuel was priest, a spiritual office. God did not allow Samuel to take over the office of king, nor did He allow Saul to take over the office of priest. Ministers are ordained of God for His service. All men are workers together for the extension of the kingdom of God. Honor God's servants so you will enjoy God's blessings on services you offer.

HOW DO YOU PREPARE TO SERVE?

Plan properly. A sales manager said, "Plan your work and work your plan, and you will be a successful man." Achievement is not accidental. Study men's lives and learn their mistakes and successes.

Take a small part first to try your ideas and skills. There are times you will do poorly or fail. Accept failure as a good teacher. Understand why you did poorly, and try again. Do not become discouraged. Do not give up.

Purpose in your heart to be loyal. Faithful attendance at church services is evidence of loyalty. Support the pastor and the programs of the church.

Refuse to find fault.

Be consistent in your daily Christian life so your testimony will be accepted by others. Ask yourself, "If every member were just like me, what kind of church would our church be?"

WHAT IS YOUR REWARD?

No thrill in life can compare with winning souls to the Lord Jesus Christ. Winning souls must be the underlying objective of everything you do for Christ and the church.

It is satisfying to know God's will and do it. If you follow God's will, you become a strong Christian who can lead others. Other laymen can be helped to become active in the church as a result of your example.

All your efforts will be more rewarded when you see Christ and hear Him say, "Well done, thou good and faithful servant" (Matthew 25:21).

I AM YOUR MISSIONARY

By Cameron W. Wilson

I AM YOUR MISSIONARY. BUT I AM DIFFERENT. You see, I do not have a wife and family to support on the mission field. For me, cross-cultural communication is not a problem. I have an amazing talent, which allows me to speak in hundreds of languages and dialects—completely without accent. I never forget an important point when telling the gospel story, and I never misquote a verse of Scripture. I am always courteous, never argumentative. In fact, I never speak to a soul unless I have his undivided attention.

I am most effective when I deal with the essentials like sin, repentance, and salvation by faith. I do not let the conversation drift into religious disputations. I do not deal in nonessentials.

I never tire of my glorious mission, and I never sleep in or fall sick. I can witness 24 hours every day—365 days a year. I shall never have to leave the mission field to go home on furlough or raise large amounts for support, medical policies, insurance, or retirement.

Even when I am ignored, I remain there patiently waiting to be noticed, read by someone who responds to my simple message and inherits eternal life.

One day, I was waiting there on the library table in Mr. Taylor's house. On that day my title was "The Finished Work of Christ." Their teenaged son picked me up, read my witness, believed, and later became Dr. J. Hudson Taylor, founder of the great China Inland Mission. If you could ask Dr. Taylor what he thinks of my work, he'd immediately answer, "I owe my life and entire ministry to the faithful witness of a printed missionary."

And there was the time I lay windblown on a street in downtown Copenhagen. There was this drunken sailor boy who noticed me there. Something made him pick me up out of the gutter, let me witness to him. He was convicted by the voice of the Holy Spirit. That day he sought out an evangelical church, sobered up, and gloriously found Christ as his Savior. In due time, he also became a missionary. Today, Christians everywhere remember that one-time sailor boy as none other than "Daddy" J.T. Back, director of the Evangelical Alliance Mission.

I am like bait which the fisherman leaves permanently in his pond. And even if I am martyred—thousands, yes, millions of paper missionaries can immediately take my place. I can easily slip behind dozens of national borders which keep other missionaries out.

If you ask about the amazing effectiveness of my ministry, here is the reason. I am the voice of God of the universe in printed form. I speak in short sentences, simple words, and easy-to-understand illustrations. Even a child can get my message. And I am actually much more than printer's ink and paper as the Holy Spirit transforms me—the printed word—to reveal the Living Word, the Lord Jesus Christ.

LFTL TOTAL INCOME

(Includes all sources of income, including foreign literature, home literature, postage, administrative, and LFTL World Ministries giving.)

YEAR	INCOME	YEAR	INCOME
1953	$ 392	1978	$ 1,309,691
1954	$ 2,163	1979	$ 1,383,197
1955	$ 3,418	1980	$ 1,559,930
1956	$ 4,733	1981	$ 1,840,741
1957	$ 5,247	1982	$ 2,232,810
1958	$ 5,652	1983	$ 2,569,121
1959	$ 8,734	1985	$ 2,756,087
1960	$ 12,937	1986	$ 2,694,652
1961	$ 16,851	1987	$ 2,989,761
1962	$ 15,414	1988	$ 3,110,786
1963	$ 31,901	1989	$ 3,298,961
1964	$ 63,870	1990	$ 3,808,843
1965	$ 70,165	1991	$ 4,155,012
1966	$116,473	1992	$ 4,088,553
1967	$189,407	1993	$ 3,932,418
1968	$189,407	1994	$ 4,083,795
1969	$250,221	1995	$ 4,346,657
1970	$352,056	1996	$ 4,655,104
1971	$349,080	1997	$ 4,893,397
1972	$437,790	1998	$ 5,650,468
1973	$498,632	1999	$ 8,024,965
1974	$631,489	2000	$10,634,906
1975	$711,284	2001	$13,270,199
1976	$892,775	**TOTAL**	**$103,191,546**
1977	$ 1,067,673		

LIGHT FOR THE LOST
CHARTER MEMBERS

John Anderson
Norman Blackman
Mat Black
Richard Black
LeRoy Bonham
Dean Burchett
Dick Carter
Roy Clanton
Sam Cochran
Cliff Collins
Glen Craig
James Cummins
Audra Friend
E.K. Griffith
I.J. Harrison
Paul Heath
R.H. Horwege
Everett James
Ben Kelterborn
Paul Klahr
Hollis Lawson
Wilbur Lyon
Homer Moxley
Alfred Nelson
Roy Sapp
Richard Schultz
Phil Sondeno
Norman Underwood
Ron Whiddon

NATIONAL LIGHT FOR THE LOST OFFICERS
1953 - 2001

NAME	OFFICE	DATE
John Ashbrook	Vice President	1996-2000
David Barth	Regional Vice President	
Glen Bonds	President	1965-1966
	Regional Vice President	
Ralph Borden	Regional Vice President	
Phil Brachler	Vice President	1974-1976
	Regional Vice President	
Bob Bruder	President	1972-1974
	Chairman	1976-1977
	President	1978-1980
	President	1984-1986
	Councilman Coordinator	1986-1988
	Vice President	1989-1993
	Regional Vice President	
Dean Burchett	Chairman	1961
David Burdine	Vice Chairman	1980-1982
	Chairman	1982-1984
Mark Burke	Vice President	1996-
Sam Cochran	Founder	1953
	National Administrator	1953-1962
	Chairman	1962-1966
	President	1966-1970
	Chairman	1970-1972
	Vice Chairman	1972-1976
	Executive Vice President	1976-1989
Ellis Damiani	Secretary	1970-1976
Benny Ferguson	Coordinator	1992-

NAME	OFFICE	DATE
Chuck Freeman	Vice President	1971-1980
	President	1980-1982
	Vice Chairman	1982-1984
	Chairman	1986-1988
	Vice President	1990-1994
	Regional Vice President	
Jerry Freeman	Vice President	1994-
Julius Fried	Regional Vice President	
James Holt	Regional Vice President	
Loyd Hoskins	Vice President	1998-
Don Jacques	President	1982-1984
	Chairman	1984-1986
	Vice President	1989-1992
	President	1992-1996
	Vice President	1999-2000
	President	2000-
	Regional Vice President	
Everett James	Secretary	1962-1970
Dwain Jones	Secretary	1979-1983
Hollis Lawson	Regional Vice President	
Joe Livesay	Vice Chairman	1986-1988
	Councilman Coordinator	1988-1989
	Vice President	1989-1990
	Vice President	1992-1996
Dr. Jere Melilli	Vice Chairman	1964-1966
Herman Meyer	Vice Chairman	1968-1972
Homer Moxley	Vice Chairman	1959-1963
Ray Neill	Regional Vice President	
Lud Oquist	Regional Vice President	
Richard Patete	Regional Vice President	
Ray Radford	Regional Vice President	
Eugene Roe	Regional Vice President	
John Slye	President	1976-1978
	Chairman	1978-1980

give me the book!

NAME	OFFICE	DATE
Phil Sondeno	Chairman	1966-1970
	President	1970-1972
	Chairman	1972-1973
Reginald Stone	Secretary	1984-1987
Bill Strickland	Secretary	1987-1992
Jerry Terry	Vice President	1995-
Charles Turner	Regional Vice President	
Tim Tyler	Chairman	1973-1976
	Vice Chairman	1976-1980
	Chairman	1980-1982
	Regional Vice President	
Len Ventling	Vice President	1992-1995
Harold Walls	Secretary	1976-1979
Otto Wegner	Vice Chairman	1988-1989
	Vice President	1989-1996
	President	1996-2000
Carroll Wilson	Regional Vice President	
Don Wilson	Training Coordinator	1984-1985
	Councilman Coordinator	1985-1986
	President	1986-1988
	Chairman	1988-1989
	President	1989-1992

For more information about Light for the Lost,
visit **www.lftl.ag.org**